Living the Dream:

Amazing Adventure in Marriage

James E. McReynolds

Minister of Joy to the World

Living the Dream: Amazing Adventure in Marriage
ISBN: Softcover 978-1-955581-34-9
Copyright © 2021 by James E. McReynolds

All rights reserved. No part of this book may be reproduced or transmitted in any form or by any means, electronic or mechanical, including photocopying, recording, or by any information storage and retrieval system, without permission in writing from the publisher.

Parson's Porch Books is an imprint of Parson's Porch *&* Company (PP*&*C) in Cleveland, Tennessee. PP*&*C is an innovative organization which raises money by publishing books of noted authors, representing all genres. Its face and voice is **David Russell Tullock** (dtullock@parsonsporch.com).

Parson's Porch *&* Company *turns books into bread & milk* by sharing its profits with the poor.

www.parsonsporch.com

Living the Dream

Dedication

To my wife Laurel

with whom I have known more joy

than I ever imagined.

My Books Published by Parson's Porch Books

2011-2021

The Spirituality of Joy: The Least Discussed Human Emotion, 2011

The Joy of Preaching: Encountering Jesus Through the Word of God, 2013

Dancing with God: A Theology of Joy, 2016

The Silence of the Church: The Spiritual Struggle with Sexuality, 2017

Spirit of Joy Church, 2019

Joy Comes in the Mourning: Love Is Forever, 2020

The Joy of the Kingdom: Envisioning the Great Commission, 2020

The Joy of Prayer: The Way to Intimacy with God, 2020

Walking with God in the Garden: Journey to Jouissance, 2021

Joy in All Seasons: Walking Each Other Home to God, 2021

Living the Dream: Amazing Adventure in Marriage, 2021

Notes on the Author's Craft of Writing

Early in life, I was aware that I had a gift for writing. My first published book was printed by Bristol Business Services when I reached the age of 17 in my hometown.

During my lifetime, I have written millions of words. I do have the human desire for appreciation of my writing. I want every word in my teaching, preaching, counseling, and writing to be useful to somebody. Rumi wrote, "When you do things from your soul, you feel a river moving in you, a joy."

I never aspired to being a tree that falls in the forest, and no one hears. I have always wanted to write. I even need to write. I want to be read as well. I want my messages to be heard. My calling to write as a public relations specialist for the Sunday School Board of the Southern Baptist Convention was a most prolific ministry. Once I told a Methodist bishop that I had written more than 10,000 articles, he laughed in disbelief. I wrote at least 750 words every day. I still do.

I am full of delight when my books hit the mark to say what Jesus would say. Who reads my projects is sometimes a mystery to me. Who needs to hear my stories? Once a writer discovers the story, she/he wants to tell, and to whom she wants to tell it, there is wordsmith joy.

I am weaker, thinner, and grayer as I become older. New writers will share their world on the saga of the ones they have loved.

My mother and a few of my friends say that I have never had an unpublished thought. I have written novels, commentaries on every book of the Bible, sermons, theology and history books, poems, books on psychotherapy, travelogues, and books on prayer, sexuality, books for children, Christmas and Easter devotionals, preaching, mental health, alcoholism, and marriage.

Writing a book, or for that matter, a sermon or a law brief, is not as easy as it looks. It is not as easy as some writers claim. One of my retired group friends frequently asks me if I am still writing. I usually respond, "Of course I'm writing. I am a writer."

Accomplished writers like John Killinger, Frederick Buechner, Ann Lamont, Henri Nouwen, Annie Dillard, Graham Greene, Thomas Merton, Rainer

Maria Rilke, Reuben Job, Perry Biddle, and a host of others inspire me to become a better wordsmith.

Reading these masterpieces help me remember things I tend to forget. I turn to their works again and again. These noted writers are my teachers. They are better writers than I will ever be. They push me to search for strong words. Their models cause me to be as clear as I can be. They push me to share the hard truth about my life. Telling old stories makes them live again. Listen to your life. See the close relationship between the excellence of the writing one reads, and the type of writing you create. Some books grace our lives. We read them in a moment when we need their words.

Pay attention to who you read when you are writing. The sensation resulting from reading and writing is like other unmerited graces. Reading best selling books on prayer is not easy as you compose a book on the intimacy of prayer from your own experience.

My wife Laurel and I start every day working the crossword puzzles. Life seems to demand it. Working jig saw puzzles is another of Laurel's morning delights.

With my INFJ personality, I can spend hours alone composing something that will help you make marriage a masterpiece, your life a joy, and assurance of your eternal home.

Laurel encourages me to write on joy. Joy is God's eternal destiny. Joy is aligning priorities with my basic beliefs. Joy is the secret of a deep connection. My wife champions my efforts. In hundreds of small ways, she makes my craft possible. I would not have written with the honesty and verve, gusto and wit without my subtle, extraordinary wife. Thanks to daughter Linda for her copyediting.

I never write a book as I wanted with words on emotions and thoughts too vast for my words. I ingest mystery, exploration, pondering on life and love and joy. Why do I write? I spent much time, energy, and money studying how to write at the University of Missouri-Columbia School of Journalism and other top educational institutions. Writing never gets you money. Writing never gets you fame. I see stories everywhere. I love seeing my words in print. To realize what I think, I must see what I say. Writers are preachers. They are curious. They are alert to details

I give my books to libraries and schools. Someday my children and grandchildren will read them. I read to them when they were small children. Writers are animated to tell stories about miracles and mysteries. Some explain their craft in books on writing. Most are bad. Even in journalism schoolteachers tell you that "you are a writer or you're not." God gives the urge and the skill. God calls and us writers must do it. Nobody writes like I do. Many write much better than me.

I enjoy doing it even if I must keep playing in the minor leagues and never make it to the majors.

Minor league writers do connect with God and others. Headlong sentences squibbed on pads or napkins create thoughts that assure readers that the writer understands how they think and feel.

Every human being has a unique story to tell. I encourage people to embrace each day, living fully with all our senses. What a joy to share the beauty in the midst of things unplanned or unexpected.

I write about topics preachers never talk about or are afraid to share. Sometimes my writing sizzles inside a person. It relieves guilt and pain. It reduces hate and anger. People are healed of anxiety concerning important things like marriage, sex, prayer, evangelism, mental health, grieving, all that creates a joy that no one really comprehends.

I write to make the connection between real life and faith. Freedom and peace replace worry and the need to be in control. As people to share their stories. Remember, we all have a story. Write on paper the moments you experienced joy. Add them to your memory bank. Read them over during difficult days. Taste life in grateful gulps. We are leaving our little marks in a big world just by being ourselves. Celebrate you that will never be duplicated. God throws a party each day because you matter. Experiencing the unconditional love of God, I want to spread it like wildfire. Read I John 4:19. I often check in with other writers who say I need to keep writing because my words do matter.

My ministry of writing includes telling stories on paper. I choose to tell stories that inform and move readers. Like a prospector with a pan following the gold, sifting facts, asking questions, I want the conversation in my writing to move my readers. Writing is one way of communication among many ways to channel my thoughts. Visit my website jamesevansmcreynolds.com to connect to readers with photos of each new book that is published to

continue the conversation, engage with other readers, and find out what I am doing next.
After writing and interacting with hundreds of couples, I find no marriage adventure is unique.

We enjoy seeing other couples refreshing their relationship. The stories are from personal experiences that Laurel, and I have shared throughout the good and bad days to a joyful contentment.

Foreword by Dr. John Killinger

This book truly is a miracle.

Dr. James McReynolds—Jim, to me, for he was one of my favorite students years ago at Vanderbilt University Divinity School. He has written many books in his lifetime, but this one is miraculous above all the others. It literally brims with extraordinary insights, wonderfully crafted statements, and incredible wisdom.

Once I started reading it, I could not stop until I had reached the last page. It was as if I were under a spell of magic, and in a way I was. I could not believe the richness of the sentences, the paragraphs, the chapters. They flowed over me like torrents of magic, page after page, from beginning to end.

The author is clearly in love with life in all its glory, and when he directs his attention to the subject of marriage, he makes the whole subject explode with glorious thoughts and expressions.

Simply thumb through the pages, glancing now here and now there, and you will see what I mean. Every page contains rich and unforgettable thoughts, statements that will be copied out again and again by other authors and will find expression in thousands of wedding sermons. They explode off the pages like a blinding array of brilliant little fireworks.

Every woman who reads the book will wish she could have been the author's wife, or at least that her husband regarded her with even a fraction of the love and devotion that fill these delightful pages. Laurel McReynolds, Jim's wife of many years, is clearly a fortunate woman, for even in her latter years she is still enjoying the wealth of devotion always seen so abundantly in her husband's thoughts and writings.

If I had had access to a book like this when I was a pastor conducting marriages. During my years at the Little Stone Church on Mackinac Island, Michigan, I performed fifty or sixty wedding services every summer. I would have made it a priority to give a copy of that book to every couple I married. I might even have given them a quiz on its contents before agreeing to conduct their wedding.

I mean that seriously, for in all the years of pastoral ministry and teaching, I have never seen another book that began to approach the subject of love as this one does. You will see what I mean as you read it. From beginning to end, it fairly bristles with glorious expressions of love and joy.

The unforgettable Norman Vincent Peale, longtime famous pastor of Marble Collegiate Church in New York City, knew what Jim was doing years ago when he credentialed Dr. McReynolds as "the Minister of Joy," for Jim's writings exude an incredible sense of joy in almost every line. This has been true in everything he has written, even years ago, but never as true as it is in this book.

The book does not deal with the easy subjects. There are chapters on sexuality in marriage and family financial matters, as well as chapters on love and romance. For many couples, there are the areas where the rub comes. But not if they can adopt the attitudes recommended by this author. Surprisingly, they too can be partners of love and positivity when viewed through the lenses provided by this book.

Perhaps what I've said sounds unduly favorable and prejudiced, but the truth is that I believe every word I've written. This is truly a remarkable book that should enrich every married person who reads it, and then tries to practice what is suggested in it. I wish I'd had it when I was a young man, but even now, in the twilight of my life, I'm delighted to read it and employ the author's suggestions in my own marriage.

Dr. John Killinger
Warrenton, Virginia

Contents

Dedication 5
My Books Published By Parson's Porch Books 2011-2021 7
Notes On The Author's Craft Of Writing 9
Foreword by Dr. John Killinger 13
Chapter One 17
    MARRIAGE: A MYSTERY TO BE LIVED
Chapter Two 35
    PLEASE UNDERSTAND ME
Chapter Three 46
    THE SPIRITUAL EXPERIENCE OF SEX
Chapter Four 60
    FINANCING THE JOURNEY
Chapter Five 69
    COMMITMENT TO IMPOSSIBLE PROMISES
Chapter Six 81
    YOU AND I, INCORPORATED
Chapter Seven 96
    SPICING UP YOUR MARRIAGE
Chapter Eight 103
    FINDING GOLD IN THE GOLDEN ANIVERSARY
Chapter Nine 116
    JOY COMES IN THE MOURNING
Chapter Ten 128
    WHEN JOY BOMBS EXPLODE
Afterword 148
Bibliography 149
Notes About The Author 156

Chapter One

MARRIAGE: A MYSTERY TO BE LIVED

God's plan for marriage is to awaken every man and woman to the spiritual journey of love: self-love, romantic love, divine love. Marriage gives the experience of the deepest of connections, intimacies, pleasures, and joys during life's journey. Good marriages don't just happen, they are made to happen. Marriages are what couples make of them. Working at marriage never leaves out the spontaneous times of fun and joy. Marriage is a lifelong creation.

It is living the dream.

Marriage is sharing your life journey with your best friend. Not having to say goodbye every night, but simply goodnight and waking to face each new day together. Marriage is a journey of learning how to make someone else happy and in that journey finding joy. Marriage is grace. Grace comes from unconditional love and forgiveness shown daily. Marriage is joy. Doing life together is fun. My prayer is that my writing this book will help you experience endless grace, joy, and love

Why is marriage such a mystery? Marriages suffer and die. A refusal to understand submission to each other and to God, selfishness, and wanting to be free from God's guidance and boundaries. With marital breakdown, feelings of inner pain and guilt goes along with it. The source of the mystery was when Adam and Eve ran away to hide from God. God desires to restore our torn bonds. Humans have missed the mystery. They lose the joy God will unlock.
The coming of Jesus brought light on all the promises of God. Read Ephesians 5. The apostle Paul identifies the spiritual nature of the mystery surrounding marriage. Paul writes that marriage is a reminder. It is love's celebration of, and a commitment to the provisions of God. The plan was to re-form the intended partnership. God desires that we navigate our life adventure together.

Paul explains the mystery with wise directives from God. Read Ephesians 5:15-20. A wholeness of living is the foundation. That involves thanksgiving, walking in the Spirit, understanding the will of God. Submission to one another as Christ demonstrated submission in its true form. Read John 17:1-5, Philippians 2:1-11.

Adventure is important as a marriage couple. Going on an adventure with your mate increases connection with feelings of invigoration and engagement with the world. Men crave adventure. Little boys play games about superheroes, knights, and dragons. Playing with passion we had as children gets lost. The thrill of excitement brings a quiet joy. Men love to show off. Men like to save and protect. Husbands are just like that.

Women yearn to be doing adventures. Women enjoy being desired and sought after by men. These are satisfied by going on an adventure together. Adventure is subjective. It does not have to be outdoors. Couples collect many things found in used bookstores. Amazing marriage adventures are about spending time together.

Your marriage may not fit the mold that my wife and I are creating. My writing helps you make a marriage that is unique to you. You will enjoy the mystery as you make the discovery of each other. Live your individual dreams. Live your united dreams. Your marriage adventure will be unique.

Comparison is the thief of joy. The moment you start comparing your partner to another relationship is the beginning of unhappiness. Each marriage is unique. Stop the comparing. Look at the positive qualities, loving the spouse for who they are. Never get serious with anyone if your only intention is to change them. Resenting a spouse for who they aren't is losing territory. To want your marriage to be like any other marriage is wishful thinking. Some women design the marriage to mean that a man must give up his calling, his current job, hobbies, and his dreams for the sake of doing life together. Another false mold is when hot chemistry ignites the fire. "I am in love" often means, "I am in lust." Men and women have unique emotional needs. Both want to be loved. Make sure you share in the deeper levels of connection that sharing life goals provide. A soul mate is a goal mate. Do you respect and admire each other? Some men and women pick people who are not emotionally safe. Feeling calm, being fully oneself, expressing yourself, feeling afraid are indicators of serious problems with the relationship.

Be on the look out for someone who is always trying to change you. Controlling and making suggestions are two different things. Suggestions are for your benefit. Control statements are only for their benefit. Discuss anything that bothers you. Fear not putting these issues on your table before you are fixed in the wrong mold. Bring up uncomfortable issues. That's the only method for evaluating how well you communicate, work together, and do healthy negotiating. Difficulties inevitably arise Before making a commitment, be certain your differences and compromises work for both of you.

Unexpected and unrealistic expectations bring misery. No two relationships are the same. Each relationship is a unique experience. Do you remember the book by Jane Austen, *Pride and Prejudice?* Five uniquely different married couples are described. Pure love was experience through characters Elizabeth and Darcy. Different attraction described the love of Jane and Bingley. A convenience marriage was that of Charlotte and Mister Collins. Financial status and their attraction and love for money was the foundational base for the marriage of Wickham and Lydia. A marriage for necessity was the kind of marriage Mr. and Mrs. Bennet lived. Austin revels through her characters in her novel on the theme of marriage. Common interests are reflected in Elizabeth and Darcy. When Elizabeth stayed in Pemberley when Jane was sick, Austin told what a unique marriage they had surrounding interests in book reading. The joyful love Elizabeth and Darcy shared is not established until the end of the book.

Your unique marriage adventure, unlike that marital life shared here, may not be a mold for others to follow.

Marriage, like life, is not a problem to be solved. It is a mystery to be lived. Marriage involves a young, energetic man falling with love for a young maiden. It's a mysterious riddle. A woman may not be mature or confident. She overlooks his immaturities and joins him. That glory
defies description. It's beauty past finding out. It's beyond understanding. Read Proverbs 30:18-19.

The element of mystery includes romance and marriage. Paul writes a classic text for husbands and wives. Read Ephesians 5:22-23. This mystery is a vital lesson for every marriage. God is the author and architect of marriage. God reveals by means of scripture the purpose and plan. Marriage is a journey together, a journey for getting to know ourselves and our other. Oneness is the goal. Couples of Greek Orthodox faith hear these words, "Master, stretch out your hand to join your servants. Yoke them in oneness of mind. Crown them in one flesh." Attaining oneness means to learn to make decisions together, not apart, and working together through the challenges and disagreements of daily living. Marriage is walking each other home. I loved Laurel on our wedding day. After these decades, I realize how limited my love for her was back then. Marriage is learning how to love each other as we discover faults or see things differently. We learn to love each other with God's love, with Christlike love. Christ's love is deeper than feelings. Feelings come and go.

The love of God is expressed as a commitment to serve and care for a special someone despite the feelings. We are to put our spouse's needs above our own desires. Saint Gregory of Nazianzus declared that marriage is the key that opens the door to discover perfect love. Christ-like love will help us o the trek toward heavenly joy. Read I John 4:12.

Get to know your own family. And plan to discover your spouses' family. Communication on these issues facilitates oneness. These must include problem solving, finance, in-laws, parenting, sexuality, faith, and personal time and couple time. Part of our communication style comes from our family. Before the wedding is the time for couples to learn how to speak and listen to each other. Effective communication builds intimacy and oneness.

The mystery is not a secret to keep. Mystery is a common word in the New Testament. Rarely does it refer to what the reader expects. Mystery remains uncertain or puzzling. Mystery is what is hidden. Mystery is not a secret to keep. Mystery is a truth to tell. Read Romans 16:25-26.

The secret was kept by God for "long ages." Until "the fullness of time" God became a human. Read Galatians 4:4, Colossians 1:26-27. Paul writes the most about mystery in Ephesians "This mystery is profound" (Ephesians 5:32) God's mystery once hidden is revealed. Mystery is profound but not something one cannot understand or express. Humans have always felt a strange pull. Pulled not just to procreate, but to commit, not knowing the reason.

Why two sexes?

Why female and male? Why the dance of two complementary souls? Is there deep magic with cosmic meaning?

God guides the holding fast, joining to, spiritual oneness with another. Marriage establishes and protects the most fundamental relationship. More than father and mother. More than the resulting children. More than a best friend. Love at first sight is understood. When two people have been looking at each other for a lifetime, marriage reveals a mysterious miracle.

Marriage is overwhelmingly joy-filled. The adventure is a gift from God to share with the person you love. Put God first. Watch God guide you. Bear each other's burdens. Make memories. Grow old together. God has an amazing track record of working with fallible humans.

The mysterious desire is to know the joy of marriage. Most people marry to young or without preparation. Discovering romance is basic. Emotional values, pleasurable rewards, sharing of work, survival. Yes. And security, mutual support, joys, responsibilities, purpose, and personal growth. Remaining single beats marriage to a wrong person. Sexual fulfillment, money, prestige, And raising children are secondary reasons. Love is never something we get. Love is giving.

Becoming a loving person is not a given. Some fear love and closeness. Some marry at the worst time. We are not ready. More growth must be developed. Circumstances must change. Enjoy life. Keep your body and spirit in shape. Don't waste your brief and valuable life.

Joy is the sound of love, the color of gratitude, and the song of hope. Joy gaps are the days between when the last time we shared joy and now.

Self-actualization may take many years. Humans travel on an invisible path. We envision dreams. We need understanding. Frustration, drama, excitement, surprise. Interesting people of the opposite sex will be encounter if we just get to know them. Some project an image. Some a false self. Share that huge world of experiences. Discover a reservoir of information. Share the rich individual talents.

Nobody knows these hidden secrets. How and who and when and what remain mysteries.

Sharpen your focus. Each person is like no other. Tastes, likes and dislikes, habits and abilities are unique. Dating a variety of personality types gives knowledge in relating to different people. Intuition leads to the type that fits you.

The joy in discovering. Fear and excitement. Quickening heart. Quivering voice. Waiting has ended. The moment has arrived. Unexpected. Reality. Never forgotten. Fully turned-on. Stay flexible. The mystery of love begins. Love adds a deeper dimension. Common becomes uncommon. Invisible realities require searching. Unmask the true self. Uncover your identity. Only then will you be ready to discover a life's mate.

Mistakes are costly. Wrong choice affects emotion, money, spirituality, and health. Be careful what you wish for. Life is impossibly risky when God reminds us how unpredictable circumstances shatter and change what we know and love about life. Like me, you enjoy making photographs of the pleasure and joy. A gaping hole is left behind s another cuts themselves out of the picture. If they had passed away, we would mourn the loss.

They feel relieved. We feel devastated. Rejection takes away the security of all we thought was stable and beautiful. Read John 12:46. We Jesus we can walk away from the dark place. All involved need to embrace Jesus. In the morning as we shallow our medication and brush our teeth, and we drink a glass of orange juice, we taste the grace. Grace erases the bitterness. I always remember the words of my supervisor at Valley Hope Treatment Center who noted "hurt people hurt people. Healed people heal people." I want to join with God on the healing side.

Marriage is a huge decision. Painful obstacles come later. To the young and naïve, getting married is incredible. Girls dream of their wedding day from childhood. Everybody wants to meet a special someone. Television shows such as, Say Yes to the Dress, causes one to imagine walking down an aisle on that perfect day. Imagination includes what the home will look like.

It is fun to dream. Some rush into marriage long before they are ready. Parents rarely approve marrying while young. They want their adult kids to enjoy youth. Some marry young and keep it a secret. Young lovers want nobody else. Settling for somebody leads to regret and boredom as the couple gets older. No matter what age marriage comes, divorce is scary. They feel stuck. Staying put or divorcing causes misery. Most young married do not know what they want.

Pregnancy pushes marriage. Pastors report that most marriage ceremonies performed include a pregnant bride. Women feel completely stuck. Life is going to be difficult. They think that getting married will make the situation better. If the groom has a good job, they believe he will provide for her and the baby. The idea of being a single mother, the thought that she does not know if she ever loved the man she married.

Another issue comes with young marrieds is the thought about seeing what is out there. Marrying a couple of years after high school means not having many serious relationships. They feel that they missed out on dating other people.

Husbands and wives must keep the channels of communication open. This helps couples face the "for better or worse" in the future. Marriage is to set sail on a beautiful but unknown ocean. It is living out life in the invisible presence of God. It is much more than being appreciated. Both are cherished. Marriage opens a couple the chance to open like a flower. They become perfectly natural, perfect selves. Marital love brings people out into the light. Love reveals. Love clarifies. Love defines. In marriage God presents us with one who strikes a deep chord than anyone else can do. Marriage enables us to find kinship in the one we love. The marriage ceremony makes it official. We have found a total stranger a near and long-lost relative. It is a true blood relative even closer than a mother or father.

All weddings are similar. Every marriage is different. During the 1987 International Singles Conference in Switzerland, I shared this letter. Joy fills my soul that I inspired them to wait on God's timing. God is the best "love story" author because God is love. During ten weeks of pre-marital enrichment at Messiah Lutheran Church in Lincoln, Nebraska, we ask each of the couples to write a letter to their future spouse. One participant wrote the following words.

"Focus on the love of God. While I am waiting, I will serve God. I will glorify my Lord through my true self. I pray we all do the same. I am saving my purity for God's choice person. By God's grace you will be the first and last commitment that I declare for any woman. Know that I loved you even before I met you."

Marriage turns a house into a home. This mystery instills a strong union. Maintain an atmosphere for joy in marriage. This takes work. Life is never easy. Struggles in life interfere with marital bliss. Take time to value marriage. Couples learn to lean on each other. Marriage is about teamwork and respect. Enjoying little moments in life come in spending quality time with each other.

Martin Luther said, "Let the wife make the husband glad to come home. Let him make her sorry to see him leave."

Dr. Seuss said, "People are weird. When we find someone with weirdness that is compatible With ours, we team up and call it love."

C.S. Lewis said, "The most precious gift that marriage gave me was the constant impact of something close and intimate, yet all the time unmistakably other, resistant, in a word, real."

Mark Twain wrote, "To get the full value of joy, you must have someone to share it with."

Maya Angelou wrote, "In all the world, there is no heart for me like yours. In all the world, there is no love for you like mine."

Marital love never goes unchanged in intensity. Working together is vital. Indifference. Animosity. Moving further apart. Marriage is fluid and changing. Remember the love when you were 16. What an overwhelming that was. Lack of sleep. Rarely separated. Undying love dies.

A new undying love replaces the last one. That's growing up. Be real.

It would be helpful to remember the times you felt rejected. Have you now perceived the good that came out of it for everybody involved? Look into the fragmented kaleidoscope of the hopes we had for love that seemed just around the corner. Our minds had run ahead in time as I dreamed of a life with a special woman. In the future we would engage in ministry together. We had envisioned snowball fights to laugh in, romantic picnics, building a house, planning a wedding, or enjoying the children.

These joys were never real for her. For me my dreams are real. My hopes were aflame. We feel that we have lost the connection to tomorrow's dream that would never be. Her words moved me. Her romantic cards and thoughts sadly brought an end in my harsh landing. God knew that this rejection would leave deep dark marks on my soul. For some of us that experience happened decades ago. The video of my memories is seen as if it occurred just yesterday.

Henri Nouwen's books line one of my shelves. He writes words that will heal any rejection or disappointment gap. "How often we tend to abide our past into good things to remember with gratitude and painful things to accept or forget. We develop a mentality in which we hope to collect more good memories than bad. Gratitude in its deepest sense means to live life as a gift to be received gratefully. But gratitude as the gospel speaks about it, embraces all of life: the good and the bad, the joyful and te painful, the holy and the not so holy.

"It is easy for me to put the bad memories under the rug of my life and to think only about the good things that please me. By doing so, however, I prevent myself from discovering the joy beneath my sorrow, the peace hidden in the midst of my conflicts, and the strength that becomes visible in the midst of my weakness.

"As long as we remain resentful about things that we wish had not happened, about relationships that we wish had turned out differently, about mistakes we wish we had not made, part of our heart remains isolated, unable to bear fruit in the new life ahead of us." (Henri Nouwen, "All Is Grace," *Weavings: A Journal of the Christian Spiritual Life*, pp. 39-40.

Scores of people have shared similar experiences. God healed my wounds. There is a scar in my soul. God uses these stories to find the ultimate good. We all cherish stability. Getting caught off guard feels like being thrown away. This book is my work to enable my readers to capture the essence of what make human rejection so awful.

Moments of joy. These times are brief. Consider your joys. Sunsets, orgasms, spontaneous joys cannot be prolonged. Marriage brings joy moments. It also experiences dissatisfying times.

Strong marriages encourage differences in tastes and thoughts. Self-fulfilled partners have their own friends experience the happiest marriages. In egalitarian marriage, there are fewer routine, repetitive elements. Enjoying the presence of an environment of possibility and imagination, keeps partners from being cynical about their relationship.

Life is not automatically exciting. Fun is a privilege for creative thinkers. If the expectation is that there will be no conflicts, disappointment results. Buried resentments and frustrations resurface. Hostility prevails. Marital life has good and bad days. Healthy fights are part of healthy relationships. Passionate romantic love will give in to a more realistic love. Illusion or magic cannot sustain a long-term marriage. We must accept the real person and give up our dreams for reality.

When women and men live together as equals, the relationship continues to improve. This creates an atmosphere where each partner feels as competent and in control of life as the other.

Monogamy does not mean boring. Mutual trust grows with time. As a couple gets better communication skills, most needs are satisfied.

Dietrich Bonhoeffer wrote a wedding sermon from his cell in 1943. He wrote it for his niece. He did not write it for publication. Bonhoeffer's letters are full of gems worth reading today. Giving is primary as a love language. For him it was family member to family member, friend to friend, colleague to colleague, and sharing love in community.

Wedding sermon from a Nazi prison. "It is right and proper for a bride and bridegroom to welcome and celebrate their wedding day with a unique sense of triumph. When all the difficulties, obstacles, hindrances, misgiving, and doubts have been, not made light of, but honestly faced and overcome. It is better not to take everything for granted. Then both parties have indeed achieved together their most triumphant.

"With the "yes" that they have said to each other, they have by their free choice a new direction to their lives. They have cheerfully and confidently defied all uncertainties with which, as they know, a lifelong partnership between two people is faced. By their own free will they have conquered a new land to live in.

"Every wedding must be an occasion of joy that human beings can do great things. They have been given such immense freedom and power to take the helm in their life's journey. The children of the earth are rightly proud of being allowed to take a hand in shaping their own destinies, and something of this pride must contribute to the happiness of a bride and bridegroom.

"We ought not be in such a hurry here to speak piously of God's will and guidance. It is obvious, and it should not be ignored. The course you are taking at the outset is one that you have chosen for yourselves. What you have done and are doing is not in the first place something religious, but, and you alone, bear the responsibility for what no one can take from you something quite secular. You have the responsibility for the success of your venture, and all the happiness and responsibility are yours.

"And the bride helps her husband to make it easy for him to bear that responsibility. You find great joy in that. Unless you can boldly say, 'That is our resolve, our love, our way, you are taking refuge in false piety. 'Iron and steel may pass away, but our love shall abide forever.'

That desire for earthly bliss, which you want to find in one another, and in which you want to find in one another, and to quote a medieval song, one is the comfort of the other both in body and in soul. That desire is justified before God and all humans.

"Certainly, you two of all people, have every reason to look back with special thankfulness on your lives up to now. The beautiful things and joys of life have been showered on you. You have succeeded in living. Each one is surrounded by love and friendship. Your ways, for the most part have been smooth. You have always been able to count on the support of your family and friends. Everyone has wished you well, and now it has been given to you to find each other and to reach the goal of your desires. You know that no one can create and assume such a life from his or her own strength, but what is given to one is withheld from another. That is what we call God's guidance.

"However, much you rejoice today that you reached your goal, you will be just as thankful that the will of God brought you here. As you confidently accept responsibility for your faithful action today, you may put it today with equal confidence into the hands of God. This day God add the divine 'yes' to your "yes,' God confirms your will with your Creator's will. God makes you instruments of divine will and purpose for you and others. With divine condescension God adds an unfathomable 'yes' to yours. God creates out of your love something quite new: the holy estate of matrimony.

"God is guiding your marriage. Marriage is more than your love for each other. It has a higher dignity and power. It is God's holy ordinance through which God wills to perpetuate humanity until the end of time.

"In your love you see only your two selves in the world. By your marriage, you link a chain of generations, which God causes to come to pass and to pass away to divine glory. You are citizens of the kingdom of God. In your loving eyes, you see the heaven of your own joy. In marriage, you are placed at a post of responsibility towards the world.

"Your love is your own private possession. Marriage is more than personal. It is an office, a status. Marriage is the crown, not merely the will to rule. Marriage is not merely your love for each other.

"As you first gave the ring to each other and today will receive it a second time from the hand of a pastor as love comes from you, but marriage is from above. As far as God is from human beings. As God is higher than we are, holy sanctity, the rights and promises come from a perfect mysterious love.

"From this day forward, your marriage sustains your love." (Dietrich Bonhoeffer, *Letters and Papers from Prison*, translation of Dietrich Bonhoeffer Werke, pp. 100-102)

"Life Together," a classic Bonhoeffer book, was published by Fortress Press. Marriage involves a formal ceremony and exchange of vows. These require commitment, an investment of time and effort. Both must see life together, closing all other possibilities. It is like a first ski run off a steep cliff in Gatlinburg, Tennessee. Scary.

Why did Dietrich Bonhoeffer return to Germany to help resist the Nazis and Hitler? This Lutheran minister, knew, like Jesus did, that he would be killed. And death came for both.

Both cling to an astonished reverence in the presence of God. What a mystery is the infinity of God! God can write straight with crooked lines. Infused with the love of Christ, we grow with more humility. God has made a promise to us. This promise is an infinite commitment. Walking with God we are redeemed. We walk each other home. The most important promise you will ever make in your entire life. The vow causes a happy nervousness. The promise between two persons brings us closer tan anyone you have ever been close to. Someone is always there to hold your hand through the good and the bad. You will stick together in oneness. Enjoying the love, the hugs, the kisses that come with love, you explode with joy.

Joy and fear walk with us at the wedding. This is quite common. Knowing the possible and impossible outcome of the marriage, it is natural to tremble. The promises are irrevocable. "I will be faithful to you until death." Each has expressed a total commitment. Time does not cancel the contract. We make these vows in a world bound by time-bound and full of sin. Both claim the joy of the Lord as the strength. God loves both of us. God is above time. Only in God will we experience the future. God embraces the present and the future. Without faith marriage freezes. Read Ecclesiastes 4:9-12.

The benefit of sharing faith is getting closer to God. We see each other through God's eyes. God and we have each other's back. Knowing that no matter what the world, the family, friends, or the church tosses toward us, we shall always have each other's back. Our souls are in God's hand.

My spiritual barometer throughout my ministry has been I John 1:4. I can measure tea munt of time I spend in the Bible by how much joy I experience. When I find a lack of joy in my life, the first thing I check is how much time I am spending in the scriptures. One evening I read Psalm 63 to my wife and family. We busted out in in impromptu songs. I continue to believe that the Bible is alive. I underline verses that speak to me on a given day. Line upon line, precept upon precept, God has guided me to live a "chaste and reverent" life.

As our theme in summer Vacation Bible School, we memorized Psalm 119:105. God's Word is "a lamp unto my feet, and a light unto my path." Bible study produces spiritual maturity, Christlikeness, for each year. As a man serving in parts of eight decades of teaching the Bible, approximately a third of my time includes time spent in prayer.

I pray before the study. I pray while being moved by what the Bible really is saying. I pray as I interpret what it means. I pray as I apply it to myself and to those to whom I'll be preaching or teaching.

After many years of study within several theological seminaries, I continue to ask God to remove preconceived ideas about portions of the Bible. People who are cultural vested in what might have been stubborn believed years ago, need to listen to the Holy Spirit who brings us freedom and wisdom in our interpretation. The agendas of liberals, progressives, conservatives and fundamentalists make wide room for error. There is always the possibility that something I have heard or studied previously has not been correct. I ask God to remove all those preconceived ideas. I pray the Holy Spirit will reveal fresh insights to me. My spirit has soared as I enjoy new thoughts from the Word. I depend upon God to enable me to be accurate and true. Jesus has assured us that the Holy Spirit will teach us all things. Read John 14:26.

When we admit our fallibility, we are teachable. Some seminary students refuse to change any of their theological understandings. Many of their ideas are built on what we think the Bible says, not what it does say. They never study or read the Bible portion before you read commentaries or helps. Unless we know first what the Bible is saying, will tend to accept the teachings in other sources. Some preachers skip through the Bible and take a verse or part of a verse to prove some point. Isolated phrases and sentences put together with a prejudiced whim can be made to prove anything.

Fallibility is acknowledging my inadequate ideas. We all live with shortcomings and sinful attitudes. Humbly seek the mind of Christ. Read Philippians 2:5-7. The joy of salvation is having the mind of Christ. All four gospels reveal the mind of Christ when he lived as a human in this world. As we feel inadequate for our spouse, for our job, we can bow as a united couple asking for the power and love of God. Love enables us to accept our inadequacy. Our attitude will change with the help of the mind of Christ. We are assured of a meek and quiet spirit. God exchanges our personalities for one of divine choice enabled by the mind of Christ.

The mind of Christ saves us from self-centered attitudes. Our emptiness is gone. We love our spouse and everybody we encounter.

The warm embrace and kindness of my wife Laurel is the heart of the defense for me and our marriage as a team. If each lives a life of worship and walks with grace, love and service is so natural. The Holy Spirit orients us to a life of blessing. Marriage provides the context in which we live that out. Marital love gets sweeter with time. A buried treasure is discovered when couples stick it out through the years.

When we love soul-to-soul it feels good. We are seen by another. The connection goes deeper and deeper into physical, spiritual, and emotional intimacy. Love lasts trough the ups and downs of life. Being authentic and confident brings trust. Marital love craves presence. We awaken unending pleasure to the edge of ecstasy. Genuine lovers desire lying together with arms and legs entangled.

A fire is ignited within. We feel the depth. Intensity. We take each other's breath away. As we stand tall, knowing our true selves, our hearts open to love. Marriage improves who we are. This sacrament helps the personal development. We become less selfish and more selfless. Some other cares for you. A lover checks-in with you. Instead of giving energy in worrying about yourself, you worry about your other one. In a successful marriage, bot bring out the best in each other. Some other supports each one's goals and passions. A partner like that helps you to become the person to dreamed of becoming.

Relationships matter. As we invest in them, we gain mutual value. When we are completely aware of this truth varies from person to person. The older I become, the more I want my limited time invested in my relationships, especially with Laurel.

It is so easy to miss the extraordinary in this ordinary world. In our ordinary lives, we must not wait for the extraordinary. Pursue it. Find it. Married life looks nothing like we imagined at the wedding. The fairytale does not fade away. Extraordinary joy will not force its way to anybody. Be converted to joy. The one lying next to you in the journey is worth the effort. The defining theme for a joy-filled marriage is offering your soul, your attention, your body, and mind. Joy is not impossible.

We give ourselves again and again. Deep connectiveness is not impossible. Marriage is not the final destination. It is a journey. Getting there. Walking together. Enjoying the adventure. Flying together. Committing to the flight. Adjusting. Dealing with delays. Not being in control. The journey is never routine.

When we are who we are, our true and best self, we experience joy. Giving up some of our personal goals and aspirations, we become open to just being aware of the love of God, our spouse, and others is possible at any moment, especially right now.

No marriage runs exactly as planned. It's forever. Committing to another until your dying day saves you from disaster. When stuck in a panic, remember your vows and Christ's promises. Jesus is the Pilot. Other couples are on the same journey that you are taking. In faith and God's strength you are headed in the same direction.

Every day can be a fresh start. In each day's new beginning, you realize that in the monotonous moments of marriage come the success of marriage. We both lay in bed thinking about what the new day would be like. We have committed to each other forever. Laurel and I still look at our wedding photos and remember how special it was.

Marriage is definitely not a destination. After the wedding, life does not end. You both are still who you are. Life is a journey, so when you marry, that is another journey. When you ride on the new journey, God and are revealed in new differing ways. Faith and trust in God's plan require reformulated faith. Faith is committing to change. The journey needs persistence. The quality of our awareness changes. Nothing shocks you. God welcomes surprises. That's the mystery and secret of living in joy.

The process is quite long as we share new knowledge. Marrieds are transformed in their joy as the enter the first phases of love before heaven. You keep moving deeper into the love of God. And God moves deeper into you both.

What did you imagine your future spouse would be like? How close is that imaginary spouse to your spouse of today? C.S. Lewis and another professor at Oxford were talking about this. Lewis said, "You and I have both known a happy marriage. How different our wives were from the imaginary mistresses of our adolescent dreams. The reality is that our real mates adapted to all our wishes. And for that reason, incomparably better."

The real never compares with the imaginary. We. Assume that means the real will never live up to the imaginary. The real person will not appear to be as good a fit in theory. The real will turn out better than the imaginary. When we dream of a spouse, we do not dream of all that we will have to overcome. We dream of battles already won. We dream of the victory, never the fight.

The reality of marriage is overcoming challenge that causes us to grow. We are vulnerable if our dream person says he or she is available for marriage. Marriage is the journey. It is not an imagined destination. In romantic lust, people act completely abnormal. Overcoming the most difficult, life changing obstacle is found in every championship season. Marriage is never sweeter than after 35 years of marriage.

Laurel is the delight of my life. It was a courageous journey to et us to this place. Marriage to Laurel has brought me the joys of her smile. We have walk each other together through some dark valleys. No couple inherits heaven immediately. To experience death is the only way we depart for the journey to heaven. Getting married does not take us there. I have preferred to travel with a lifelong companion, even one who is not perfect. Laurel completes me. She makes everything better. She is more than any imaginary spouse would have been.

Fantasy spouses do not exist. Every relationship strength comes with a correspondent weakness. The fun woman may be a little too irresponsible. That is the reason we need to die to the fantasy of arriving in order to begin the journey of becoming. Until you come to desire the real more than you do the phantom, you are not re to commit your life in a marriage. You must accept your spouse's weaknesses as you receive strengths. Read Thessalonians 5:11. Every spouse will eventually break down.

Only real marriage urges us into mysterious unknown waters. The natural inclination is not toward love or depth in a relationship. If we know marriage's great miracles of grace, we must go against the grain of fallen human nature. Our own limited devices are devastating. Like life itself, it is a mystery to be lived. To marry is such a staggering decision that many would not enter it. This lifelong encounter is more vigorous and demanding than we would ever choose, desired, dreamed of, or invented by ourselves. Jesus indicated that to be with God in heaven is to be married to God and all God's children. Earth marriages are a pale image compared to the joining God with the groom. We are the bride. Holy Scripture often uses the picture of a wedding, of a bride and groom, to convey what it means for human beings to be united in love to God. We love others as we love ourselves. Jesus made it clear that God loves humankind so intimately that the Divine wants to marry them.

The wondrous surprise of the original marriage in Eden takes place again. This joy is sheer amazement. All people are related. We are all bound in love. God and we experience a divine pondering. The new Eden is beyond imagination. Love comes embodied with flesh and bone. The are walking, talking, and are on a journey walking each other home. That is the mystery of marriage life. Living under the same roof with another human being who has been a stranger. Knowing this person better than anyone in the world. Sometimes you wonder if you know them at all. That mystery of strangeness increases with the security of the other's embrace. No one else will ever love us like God does. We seek to love the children of God the same way.

That strangeness we feel with the other indicates the measure of the closeness of God. What a wonder that this closeness comes in a committed marriage. Love makes choice and free will, possible. We choose our highest good, even in our natural human inclinations.

Communicating these truths will be a harbinger to life in heaven. Even if we are bogged in the wrong problem, God will guide us with exactly the right answer to our need. This is the mysterious supernatural process of the Spirit who never makes an error.

Joyful marriages bring Christ into it. God has spoken to married couples for all ages and places.

Read Acts 2:42. The mysteries of oneness are lived by our commitments. God gives guidance with love. That love is a yardstick of perfection. Doing marriage God's way is to behold our faces in a mirror. We immediately change our marriage and we become blessed persons. We find the mystery is that marriage is not a mystery to be solved, but a life to be lived in the joy of the Lord.

I often quote and look at Saint Francis' famous prayer of the 12th Century, "Make Me an Instrument of Thy Peace."

"Lord, make an instrument of thy peace.
Where there is hatred, let me sow love,
Where there is injury, pardon,
Where there is doubt faith,
Where there is despair, hope,
Where there is darkness, light,
Where there is sadness, joy.
"O divine Master, grant that I may not so much seek
To be consoled as to console,
To be understood as to understand,
To be loved as to love,

For it is in giving that we receive,
It is in pardoning that we are pardoned,
It is in dying to self that we are born to eternal life."

Quoted in James McReynolds, *The Spirituality of Joy: The Least Discussed Human Emotion*, p. 249.

One sure indication that you have lost your joy instinct is that you are experiencing less cheerfulness, less positive affect. Jouissance is rejoicing in all that you are, all that you have, and all you have the potential to be. Living in a marital relationship means to learn to live with another through all the bliss and pain that married people experience. It is a daring adventure. It requires sacrifice, a joyful heart, humility, and obedience.

Chapter Two

PLEASE UNDERSTAND ME

The first days of marriage are exciting and threatening. The masks are dropped. Communication is a life-long process. As we reveal ourselves and learn who this person really is. As we drop the protective masks and allow each other to know who we really are, the goal is to please understand me. Some relationships are deceptive. The real self is hidden. We are afraid to disclose who we are. When was the last time you looked into each other's eyes to enjoy an intimate conversation?

Communication is the core of any marriage. Understanding each other will rekindle your passion. What if you needed medical treatment for survival? Less dramatic is the marriage adventure leasing to contentment and joy. Make communication a priority. Put your multi-tasking aside as you get the benefits of your quality time of conversation. Be proactive. Narrow your focus. Focus on the moment.

"The only true discovery would not be to visit strange lands, but to possess other eyes, to behold the universe through the eyes of another" is insight from Marcel Proust. Communication involves an awareness that understanding each other is not a simple task. I live on a strange island. My wife lives on another island. Neither of us can swim. We share keeping our own true selves and uniqueness.

Understanding each other by "possessing their eyes" or "walking in their shoes" is to practice empathy. We must understand another's perspective to see into another's emotions. Differing definitions and measures of perspectives are used. We try to discover the other's beliefs. Beliefs can mismatch skills. Even if and when human beings know themselves, our perspectives are skewed by one's social desires. Shifting into another's viewpoint involves the "please" in understanding. Everyone has what they think is a clear perspective on their empathy.

Paul Tournier says most people are poor listeners. "Each one speaks primarily I order to set forth their own ideas. Few exchanges of viewpoints manifest a real desire to understand the other person." (Paul Tournier, *To Understand Each Other*, p. 4) Two great listeners are needed for one marriage. We feel love when another understands. Misunderstanding becomes serious when one person regularly fails to respond to the other's plea to please understand me.

All couples will experience disagreements and emotional exchanges. Even the best marriage adventure will include fighting. Some fight more than others. It is a way of life for many couples. Realize that spouses will fight occasionally. Do not wait until the heat of the moment before you communicate some rules for engaging in conflict. Counterproductive and hurtful fights occur if you do not set rules for conflict now while both are calm and are content in each other's company. The goal is to resolve an issue. It is not to hurt the one you love. Couple strive for two winners. With understanding and compromise, healthy and marriage-oriented communication is always the possibility.

Here are some suggestions. Look into each other's eyes when communicating during a conflict. Ignore distractions. Focus on solving the problem. Avoid side issues. Guard your tongue. Do not bring up any history of disagreements. Hold hands. Finish talking about the conflict. The issue will fester if you finish feeling angry, ridiculed, or in continuing negation.

Spend some time to establish some ground rules for future fights. Some issues are off-limits. Behaviors and actions that are cruel and unproductive are known by each partner. How open are you for compromise? Can you walk hand to hand without seeing eye to eye? Take your rules-making to a calm time. Laurel and I realize that we have moved out of bounds, we say, "We are not fighting fair." That may be the clue if you feel awkward about handling conflict when you are not angry.

Instead of imagining ourselves in another person's position, we need to gain their perspective. We assume that another person thinks and feels just as we do. We tend to use our own perspective to understand other people. Ours is not their perspective. We imagine how the other feels about getting fired. Imaging how they feel about our jokes, our political views, our spiritual insights. In fact, we are thinking of how we would feel in their situation.

Imagining another's perspective will not improve our understanding of how another thinks or feels. When people risk talking and listening before making predictions concerning them. Understanding another person's perspective through conversation increases the accuracy of understanding. It is only possible when we probe them about what they think, rather than assuming we already know. We cannot rely on intuition for insight. Please listen. Listen again and again.

Getting an accurate perception allows finding new information about another person. To understand what your marriage partner prefers, ask. Don't just guess. Ask.

God asked, "Why are you hiding?" in the Genesis story. God was seeking Adam and Eve's perspective. He was trying to understand them.

The good news is that God accepts us as we are. By the grace of God, our mate can accept us as well. Communication means in communion with. Never rip off the other's mask. Give patient freedom and space to drop the mask. Enjoy what they offer. Faith in our own commitment with commitment of the other to unity and permanence gives freedom to reveal innermost thoughts.

Understanding each other is a gradual process of sharing daily routines. Communication is a journey into the inner space of each other. It involves mystery, an ever-changing kaleidoscope that fascinates, attracts, and intrigues. The mystery can never be fully known. Withdrawing and refusing to reveal ourselves diminishes love.

Avoid interruptions. Put the cell phone in another room. Speak freely. Listen better. Feel the impact. Maintain eye contact. Break the ice. Create a love environment. Life feels thankless. We run from task to task. We meet daily obligations. The energy we use is taken for granted. We appreciate all that is done. We would be lost if it were not for each other. Don't overlook the little things. We have routines such as cooking, cleaning, taking the trash out, and paying the house monthly billing. We need to express our thanks.

The multitude ways we can misunderstand demonstrate just how complicated it can be to understand each other. It is an illusion that couples can live in the same house for years and not really understand each other. Listen for the meaning of spoken words as well as the feelings.
We listen with our whole bodies. Listening is an active process. We respond verbally and non-verbally. Avoid interruptions.

Effective communication in marriage identified. When we are "in love," communication comes naturally. We deliberated work at it. We row upstream. Keeping at that rowing keeps us from going backwards. People drift. How do they close the gap? Without communication aimed to understand, there can be no relationship. Communication builds a bridge for moving toward each other.

Upon the first meeting, communication is reduced to the essentials. We share facts that are safe. We talk about people or events that are obvious.

Communication goes deeper as we share about what we think. This could be threatening or a reason for rejection. Distinguish conflict from quarreling. Quarrelling is a negative word.

That type of communication means being angry and showing it with loud outburst. It is never a gracious way to communication during a conflict. Conflict is inevitable. Quarreling need not be a base for communicating conflict.

Communication gets bolder as we show feelings and emotions. This vulnerability rarely brings rejection. It brings a new closeness and intimacy. As we find more understanding, unconditional acceptance brings the contentment and pleasure. Any relationship will naturally grow.

Understanding each other involves speaking and listening. Practice is needed. It is a two-way process. Somebody summed communication in these words. "I know you believe you understand what you think I said, but you don't know if you realize that what you heard is not what I meant."

Oneness involves our heart and our minds. Effective marital communication joins together analytical understanding and our emotional heart commitment. Academic settings are where I came to understand Christian faith. Christian brothers and sisters who stay exclusively in the thinking area may not be understand. Things in the mind are brain acts that may not connect to the heart. Couples must consider other options to be fully understood. Spirituality is not just intellectual, but it also comes through our hearts. Take the things you know and allow your heart to encounter them.

Those who think we must use analysis to find the content and form of the Bible, are not free to seek the Holy Spirit I our understanding and communicating what the Bible attempts to say. That trusting brings an appreciation inside the heart. We need a balance for wholesome understanding. We keep searching for the truth. We always need improvement. We welcome the opportunity to be closer to God. The process will never be completed in this life. Those who have been walking an exclusive analytical road, need to walk with God in a more understanding and closer way.

Couples can be committed to Christ Jesus and still not feel close to God. Those who are reading this book gain an understanding about the joy of the Lord found during life's journey. If you bought this book for intellectual understanding, you will be disappointed. Feel deeper as you read each chapter. I would be grateful if you read the thoughts as a couple. Organize a book club or church group to read and discuss it together. I do believe the story in this book will make a difference. Use your mind and emotions together.

Life is full of hurts, losses, problems, and challenges that have possibilities for feeling the presence of God. The difference between understanding the concepts in this book. Feeling these concepts is the difference between analyzing and experiencing love.

Practicing our spirituality is like that. God is real and we know it when our hearts and minds join in oneness. Read II Thessalonians 2:13. Some are blown away by every interpretation or theological aberration that is current. We need grace and truth together.

Silence kills understanding. Speak about what you are feeling and thinking. Do not resort to exaggeration. Avoid global statements such as always or never. Speak only what you understand as the truth. Tone of voice and body language speak volumes. Communicating with love means to help not hurt. Some make truth a weapon.

Active listening is the most neglected aspect of communication. Listening is a skill that needs to be cultivated and learned.

Let me share how to identify and evaluate listening skills. Think of a person to whom you enjoy talking with. Make a list of the reasons you like talking with this person. List what this person does while you are talking.

Now think of a person to whom you find it difficult to talk. What does this person do that makes it difficult to talk?

Evaluate listening skills. List the things you try to do to make it easier for another to talk with you. List things another does to make it easier for you to talk to another. List some things that you would like another person to do that would make it easier for you to talk.

As you share these lists, tell the other two things on each other's list that you are going to try to do this week beginning now.

To communicate we must tune in. This is not a natural trait. Active listening is not passive. Focus in at the exclusion of everything else. Turning to face the person helps. Get rid of distractions. Shut down noises that limit clear hearing. Listening is showing respect. Two porcupines nestling together is a metaphor for the barriers we build.

Laurel and I share an office in our home. Now retired, we spent a lot of time together. We stop and drink coffee. We create our environment for talking and listening. When your spouse cries out, "Please understand me," loving communication dodges misunderstandings. Beliefs, norms, values, standards vary. Differences cause misunderstanding. Both will view extended family, roles, finances, attitude toward work, sleeping, alcohol use, leisure time as being what is normal.

Communication is the key to everything in life. Marital breakdowns in communication can bring a marriage down. The essential thing is that people want to be understood. They desire to feel like their emotions are being valued. If that does not happen, there are marital problems. A simple note, a text message, or a vocal compliment results in being appreciated. Each feels validated and understood. Each spouse needs support. That is positive reinforcement.

Talking and listening require knowing, acknowledging, Effective communication is not a mystery. Examining the true self comes with each suggestion. We compare our real behavior with ideal standards. Shape your words to the person who listens. Let your spouse become the true focus. The whole body reveals the message. That message is not just information. During the crowded words of talking, speak your mate's name. The conversation that began as his has become yours. Wisdom is the ability to listen.

We re-learn listening on the marriage journey. We develop freely into the likeness of each other. We are not deterred from growing into the likeness of Christ.

Our growth reveals individuality not as something to be grasped. Our true soul is a gift from God. Within a living relationship, we discover ourselves through the reciprocity with others. Existence is not only in ourselves, but in relation to God. God is a marriage. The family of God is not ashamed of being like each other. We love another person enough to become like them.

Marriage brings a small glimpse of the mystery of God bearing our sins with the birth of Jesus.

What if we are the ones to cry, "Please understand me." If you have dared to open in the past, only to be misunderstood, you are now tensing up. It's too scary to go there. Maybe your communication was not the way of God in Jesus. Love travels on the communication pathway. Communication is not something we are born with. Skills are needed. We are capable of learning how to be effective.

Listen with your heart, not just your head. Read Ephesians 4:9. Serving as a director of nursing means supervising nurses and medical workers. Laurel directed the work of 300 people in five locations. Often as she shared her stressful days with me. These times were lessons in communication. I tried to validate her feelings. She usually wanted my understanding about how this made her feel."

Understanding each other enriches love and friendship. Intimacy grows deeper day-by-day. We become intimate with intimacy. Intimacy means different things to each couple. Poor communication unconsciously pushes us away. We are intimate when we reveal our real selves.

We would not ordinarily reveal parts of our inner self to the average person on the street.

Intimacy happens on differing levels. It does not require two people to be intimate. One person is intimate and the other one witnesses it. Sharing secret thoughts are powerful moments. I allow my other to see into me. When that happens, we find commonalities that appears as destiny. Communication like that looks like a miracle. Laurel and I laugh at the same things. We are vulnerable as we find each other's fragile places. Intimacy happens in sharing emotionally. The dancing of mutual unveiling stops at the shallow levels.

The risk in communication becomes bolder. Love involves people revealing the center of their existence. We can admit that we are weird. Weird is good. Remember you choose a mate that you will enjoy talking with all the days of your life. Tell your spouse the things that were so special, things that warmed your soul. Let them understand what this means to you. Affirmation is a key. We become much better spouses. We acknowledge the smallest effort.

Becoming elderly is a new thing in history. Most never were able to live the biblical three scores and ten years. Old people received much greater respect when there were not so many of them. Images have historically been negative. The Hebrew Bible pictures what the aged can expect. Gray hair. Loss of eyesight. Loss of hearing. Loss of potency. Lack of enjoyment. Today we can remedy most of these negatives. The perceptions of old people are more positive than the perceptive projected upon them by younger people. False understanding and perceptions are not shared by most older people I know. Lonely. Rigid. Narrow-minded. Ineffective. Finished. Old age is a puzzle that we tend not to put together. Far from being rigid or finished, most are bursting with life, enjoying the discoveries of themselves and God. Attitudes can be changed if older people live among those of every age. The positive result would be a profound acceptance of our human condition.

Memories compensate for our losses. Memories connect scattered parts of our puzzles. Reconnecting with another brings delight, wonder, and engagement that keep relationships alive. Remembering rejuvenates to inspire fresh creativity. Memories affirm each other's work. They affirm our worth. Memories take us to our favorite places. They highlight accomplishments. To be solidly rooted in the world, we own and share our histories.

People are always in process. We are constantly being changed. Sharing each other's on-going story completes the life picture and our becoming. Older people are described as wise. Wise folks have a solid sense of self. They come to realize what life is about. Ambiguity. Undoubtedness. Contradiction. Substance, not trivia. Compromise. Lifted. Embraced. Insight. Knowledge. Wisdom.

Stereotypes may accurately define some older wise ones. They are never symbols for all. God's precious old wise owls live in the present moment. They are opened by deep longings. The live by the lure of God. This is faithful and wise aging.

Ask people in your life to share some spontaneous thoughts about old age. Compare words, messages, and images about older people. We and other institutions such as home and church need to respect and incorporate older people to produce a more-age-inclusive, healthier society.

God exchanges a presence for loneliness. God gives lost power for our weakness. Healing for illness. Hope for despair. Peace for anxiety. Love for resentment. Comfort for sorrow. Grace for suffering. Couples are not surprised that there will be conflicts. As I was hiking on the beautiful Blue Ridge mountains in southwest Virginia, two mountain streams merged with sound and sight of the crashing of swirling waters. When couples merge into oneness, they are like surging, bubbling of streams, our goal is to produce the same results.

Let me share one of my experiences. The names, locations, or any way for identification has gotten my personal effort. A man named Bubba John now enjoys a balance between his head and his heart. Bubba John was brought to his knees. He had a short marriage lasting just a few months. He thought is spouse was the woman of his dreams.

Everything that could go wrong went wrong. The encounter with her was a disaster. His self-esteem was shattered. His faith sank into the depths of depression. All we knew about spirituality seemed irrelevant. He neglected prayer. He had prayed for life with this woman. God appeared not to be listening. Going to church became just one more burden. He did realize that he was a child of God. He struggled to find the joy of his salvation.

A hymn, "I Know Whom I Have Believed," triggered God's filling his heart with new strength.

Peace and love wrapped around him. Tears flowed from his eyes. Jesus quietly touched Bubba John. "The joy of the Lord" remained with him. He picked up loose ends with God's joyous strength.

He trained and received a job in an alcohol and drug abuse treatment center. With another believer who worked with him, he met with him in prayer. When there was a dramatic change in a patient, a supportive staff member would catch Bubba's eyes and smile. The same God who has touched the lives of multitudes of people is ready to come into your life.

Because we each have our own unique backgrounds, we have different ideas about communication. Getting conflicts out in the open helps us understand each other. Confrontation is not a synonym for blowing your stack. Read Proverbs 25:11. Good communication is the beginning of finding a satisfactory solution. Sometimes the best solution is to accept it. Compromise. Both of you can be winners as compromise. Compromise anything but the relationship.

I like that term oneness. I use it often. A successful marriage is not free of trouble, but with oneness couples can prepare for it. Read Romans 8:28. Paul is not saying that all things are good. Find the good in all that enters our story. Your marital adventure is yours for better or worse.

Couples experiencing the impact of a crisis, keep trying old patterns of marriage that worked in past generations, but not now. Marriage is not a state to be achieved. Marriage is not a product.

Marriage is a process based on reality. Laurel and I suggest a model for moving on with the adventure despite adultery, bankruptcy, unsafe expressions of feelings, a design for building and rebuilding a marriage. These human crises contain the root for opportunity. Nothing is just a breakdown, but a breakthrough. Now, couples can create a new pattern. Couples are facing future shock. We see a change and maturity. Guilt and blaming, religious rules, Spouses no longer want a spouse to be dependent on them. After years of marriage and family therapy, many family life conferences and retreats, up to date continuing education, and acceptance of where we are today. Each marriage is a new unique union. We stress the opportunity for independence, equality of power, acceptance, responsibility, and freedom of choice.

Marriage is broader than a mere legal term. Attempting to live responsibly together, with the welfare of both taken into consideration with a commitment to the future regardless of the past.

This book aims to help spouses understand each other. I pray couples will use this information as a frame of reference to evaluate your unique situation, find out where you are in the process, understand the dynamics and communicate techniques appropriate for marriage.

Couples are human and problems will continue. Each has individual and conflicting needs, feelings, and desires. Each views the world from the perspective of their families of origin.

There is a better way. Couples must accept that no marriage is perfect, neither are the people involved. They need to learn the process of a satisfactory marriage. They must take charge of the relationship. They must communicate how to comfortably be living together.

No matter how ugly life has been, feeling satisfied and fulfilled is possible. The picture I paint with the words in this book provides information to move the marriage on to fresh and more satisfying levels.

Each person communicates a unique fantasy dancing through the head. Both think theirs is real and that the partner should think the same way. Both are unaware and they say, "Please understand me. Let me hear what I want to hear and let me see what I want to see." Maintaining the fantasy is the prime concern. All energy is directed to achieve the goal. Couples learn to use words to manipulate each other to match their fantasy.

The positive aspect is that they never progress without a dream. Even if the marriage is continuing at the skin of its teeth, we encourage couples to be together to build a new solid base. They need this time to find a possibility for created a loving relationship. Their power struggle is overt and moves into uncomfortable fights with each other. Each one struggles for the marriage to proceed as they now envision it.

Each individual need not be perfect. To bridge the gap requires each one accepting the imperfection. Each one finds freedom from fear that the other person will discover a flaw. That will only ruin the fantasy. The fantasy is now joyfully relinquished.

Each party is an adult. They have full knowledge of the situation. They can now form a marriage contract that will create the sort of relationship that both are pleased with. Awareness of the reality of the relationship is important so that choice can be maintained. The ideal is to be consciously choosing what we want life to be. Life is a movement. Movement requires change. To grow in living, change is necessary. Patterns of how couples communicate can develop along lines of safe areas. Couples can choose freely to do something to improve their situation or to leave it as it is. Living a dream life is wonderful if you have enough energy to maintain it. Less energy is required to stay in an unrealistic fantasy.

A more positive use of energy is to do reflective listening with the unwilling spouse. Reflective listening is acting as a mirror reflecting the sense of what the spouse is saying, not adding anything new.

Moving out of the emotional fog, reflective listening helps to become clear. Feedback is needed as each describes the behavior rather than inferences about the underlying motivation. Tell how you experience this behavior. Avoid making interpretations. Never try to tell your partner what is going on inside her or him. Interpretations are projections. In order to stay married, we need to be here now. Put down the past and the future and be present in the relationship with understanding and effective communication.

Chapter Three

THE SPIRITUAL EXPERIENCE OF SEX

Sex is purely physical. We hear that all the time. "Love is a feeling. Sex is a sport."

Nobody can love you like I can. Don't you wish your girlfriend could give sex like me?"

Purely physical excitement entices affairs or conquering someone else's spouse is biologically driven. The thrill of unforgettable love burns in the skin. Initial lust passes. Glow recedes.

Sex is easy. Intimacy is difficult. Finding an intimate, trusting, committed relationship means to know and fully be known. Not like instant oatmeal, oneness is not automatic. Intimacy is an oyster that has a shell to protect. Intimacy is a spiritual adventure. It demands significant self-investment. Intimacy is vulnerability that coaxes us to join with another person. Intimacy shared in the amazing adventure of marriage fills us like nothing else imaginable. Living a dream, like all of life, comes to a physical end.

Our wildly mysterious sexual God designed sexuality. Nothing is more silenced in churches than the unlocking passionate enjoyable sex in marriage. God desires humans to know passion in sex.

Church people have their lips locked. One task in marriage is to get rid of the false videos playing in our heads. To produce new videos, people must stop pretending that hiding hopes, dreams, wishes, and feelings protects us from rejection or the pain of lost love. The connection is spiritual. It is inside us.

The driving force is our need for intimacy. We are born alone. We die alone. From birth to death, we search for genuine intimacy. We confront our inner-self critic before passion unfolds. Mind-reading restricts flexibility. Without emotional and spiritual exposure, there is little connection. The unknown stimulates new excitement. A change in the setting stirs love's embers. Stretch past your security zone. Remember the poetic verse, "Keep not your roses for my dead cold brow. Let me know love now." Fear keeps couples from living God's dream for them. Fear of vulnerability. Fear of change. Fear of the uncomfortable. Fear of responsibility. Fear of the unknown. Fear of disapproval.

The words we use about sex, and those we avoid usually reveal our attitudes to it. There is no way we escape expression of our values. To ignite your lover's passion, you need passion of your own.

The way to joy in life is to embrace a positive view of sex. We underestimate the toll on intimacy and the survival of marriage. Where, with whom, what, when, and why are perceptions from awareness of sexuality from others in society, sexual abuse, ignorance false mind videos, and in tragic circumstances. Views about sex are mostly negative.

In 2017 Parson's Porch Books published my book, *The Silence of the Church: The Spiritual Struggle with Sexuality*. AJ Beaber wrote the foreword. Let me share part of what she wrote.

"This book is a bold proclamation from a courageous pastor, willing to break the silence and speak about joy still found in sexuality and the church. It challenges congregations everywhere to open their platforms and ministries to discuss this important subject, one that deeply affects our households and future generations.

"Here one will discover a voice for sexuality from a spiritual perspective to fully embrace our sexuality as a gift from God."

Some churches teach that sexual promiscuity before marriage is "the unpardonable sin." Some refuse communion. They cannot believe that they deserve enjoyable sex in marriage. They keep thinking that God is punishing them. Sexual sin is not beyond reach. Walk with each other in God's forgiveness. See sex in the positive light of love.

Miserable people view sexual pleasure as always wrong. God says sexual pleasure is holy and full of joy. I wrote my book on sexuality because there is so much abuse and sexual sin that the destruction of passionate sex with the one God chose for you to love in the safety of marriage needs healing.

Sex is physical. And spiritual. And God honoring. God created sex and called it good. There is an entire book in the Bible about sex. The Song of Songs was included. God shows us eternal love, including sexual intimacy. Read Song of Solomon 5:1. The Word tells us to get the full amount of pleasure from the experience. By exploring sensations of touch, we can discover more about sexual feelings. We grow in self-confidence by becoming aware of our human needs. Few start off entirely confident. We learn it with positive experience When we love someone, we desire to give ourselves entirely. It is beautiful to lose our own self to find ourselves.

The Song of Songs is written as an illustration of marital passion. It uses metaphors and allegories. Read Song of Songs 4:1, 4, 6. This Old Testament book gives spot on interpretations of sexual passion. It is a passionate description of profound love.

Assertiveness in sexuality means entering into a covenant by expressing how you feel in a constructive way. God has designed the whole body as an erogenous one. We come alive with the right touch. Pure intimacy. Closeness. Shared fun.

Church people fear sin. Prohibitions abound in the church. Humans suspect human desire. Devote and devout married people fear sexual passion. Love is twisted within them. Guilt taints everything. Their fundamental sexual behavior has no ease, no variety, no fun. Personal pleasure is self-indulgent. A conservative and squinting religion unsexes them.

Sexual intimacy between husband and wife is a metaphor for our relationship with God.

Becoming one flesh is like the relationship of love between Christ and the church. Humans are never closer physically than when entwined in sex. Sex becomes most intimate when we bring God and love into the marriage bed. By itself, sex is really a physical act. Sex is an expression of closeness. It is a most private, covenant love. In sexual union a couple discovers the deeper meaning of loving and being loved. Sex comes as serendipitous gifts. Sex is spiritual. It is the quest for union. Beyond the human conscious mind, it is way past all realms of previous imagination.

When people who are not committed to each other practice sex, they have no personal desires for the other. If the sex is labeled as unsatisfactory, they run. There is no room for the presence of another human being. Dominating sexuality does not produce love. In marriage, sex either excludes or includes the other. The value and the joy of lovemaking is that it is never finished.

Building the total relationship is required. Not all sexual episodes will be the same. Steamy and hot, at other times slow, lingering, and quiet. Jesus did tell us that there would be no marriages in heaven, he did not rule out the fact that we would be identified as male and female. The sexual distinctions will continue in our eternal place. When two married people experience oneness in their coupling, they confirm the images of being male and female. Not every married couple will experience sizzling, athletic sex. Mutual satisfaction and fulfillment arrive without the fizzle.

When couples see beyond the physical, they will cultivate a positive attitude toward this gift from God. Being in tune with the broad meaning helps in the physical aspects of marriage. We long to fully know what sexual really means. It is the linking of two people in oneness. Before being physically bound, we are emotionally and spiritually united. Ordinary exterior relations become intimate revelations. That is a promise for those who seek it.

Yellow is the color when I think about my wife Laurel Ann. She is optimistic, bright and cheerful. Being with her is like living in a home of sunshine. Our oneness grows like a house plant when couples create an environment for total unity. Closeness never comes with smothering, but by uniting in a unique blending that pays respects for everyone.

Union of intimacy is partial. The sense of communion is realized as two are joined deeply. Each maintains their individuality. Being a separate self is indispensable. Love brings an atmosphere for sharing. The atmosphere is one of freedom. Marriage is a free fusion, not confusion. The more personal we feel free to share, the more exciting the relationship bursts open in joy. All relationships have ups and downs. The amazing adventure include times when the fires of love burn brightly. At other times, the embers glow more faintly. Intimacy has its ebbs and flows.

Peaks and valleys leave couples uncertain, but those committed to their connection cope. Hanging in there during lean times is realized by having appropriate role models for intimacy.

Sex does not create a quick fix. Easy answers cause heartache. Our souls seek a love beyond what we have ever known. We quest to go beyond common love. Each effort prepares us for the next step. Dive deeply. Discover the extraordinary power of love. The depth, strength, and quality of the love relationship is the picture of any intimate relationship. We must navigate every up and down. We need to be vulnerable. With that openness, comes the possibilities and pleasures of love. Our beings connect. Souls unite. Bodies dance. Ecstasy. Joys. Challenges become connections. Conflicts become communion. We are invited deeper into the most sacred part of love. Love transcends all things to unite two as one. Read Proverb 31.

Some marriages are plagued by chronic illness or factors that means a sexless marriage. Some go years and years without sex. Imagine the resentment. No physical soul mingling. Passionate sex stirs up amazing grace. Lacking sex, distance damages the oneness. We are in this together. Long periods without love damages the shared joy, deep friendship, and vulnerability. Sexual desire does not mysteriously leave the adventure. Passion does not leave us. We leave passion.

The demand of fidelity unsettles any spouse. In our promiscuous and unfaithful society, few marital relationships this side of Eden have remained faithful. Avoiding sexual contact with a third person brings trouble. There are no stereotypes, simply because each person is unique. Every married person must shape fidelity within their own marriage. People are smart enough to realize that extramarital sex is adultery. They are not prepared to brand all adultery as wrong.

We rationalize it, we must live with the fact that all human beings do move outside of marriage for sexual experiences. Research by Kinsey's team reported that 70 per cent of married men interviewed admitted to having had extramarital sex. Some experts today say it's even higher.

No wonder it is such an important issue. Most people and institutions remain silent. Why?

Some just label it all as lust and degeneration. The expectation is simply to throw off restraint and follow fleshly desires. Nobody is a stranger to lust. Still most people want to know why. Reasons for adultery are as varied as adulterers. Each reason is interconnected. There are fewer and fewer props in this world to prevent adultery. Neighbors used to care. They stayed on watch. Society erected fences for lust and sexual needs. Churches threatened and admonished. Family and friends frowned. Pregnancy was then a huge possibility. There were no pills or means of prevention. Movies and media never urged the consideration of our sexual desires. We all now live in a sexualized atmosphere. Men and women meet each other on a free and equal basis.

People make more money than ever. They can easily pay for secret lunches and drinking alcoholic beverages. We have easy access to hotel rooms. We can easily go to places where the secrets are not out in the open. Beware. The chances of getting caught are practically possible.

Without physical and emotional intimacy, we become mere roommates sharing resources and chores. Marriage and sex were designed by God. It is futile to write thoughts like "an ounce of prevention" or "affair proofing" a marriage. A feisty spouse hungering for sex may be tempted to loosen their vows. Refused spouses convince themselves that indiscretion. Few even call the cheating adultery. Division is easy when unity is not cherished. Sexual desire must be tamed with masturbation. Enticed with pornography becomes alluring. Most desperate viewers have been consistently rejected in that area of pleasure.

Sex as an uncontrollable urge is present in most of the cases ministers, therapists, psychiatrists, and psychologists work with. The problem extended far and wide with more people involved than imagined. For lovers with addicted passion, love possesses them. They do not know why. Professionals, well-known people including presidents and politicians, and unknown regular people become involved. At the heart of the problem is love as passion, a biological or unconscious state activated by irrational appeal.

Passionate love is the state of intense longing for union with another. Reciprocated passion is rationalized brings fulfillment and ecstasy. Sexualization of the relationship involves being preoccupied and thinking about the person being seduced. Idealization of the other stimulates the desire to know and be known. Positive feelings come when things are going well. The desire is for union. Actions such as pumping up each other's ego bring on feelings. Passionate love is like any other form of excitement. Vulnerability. Anxiety. Panic. Despair. Calmness. Euphoria. Happiness. Secrets. The risk of revealing the sexualized relationship adds fuel to the fire. The term "passionate love" is any intense longing for union with another. The presence of the lover is an aphrodisiac. Sight. Smell. Sound. Touch. Stimulations for desire. "The better to seduce you with, my dear." The excitement is confusing. Both are aroused.

Undeserved love is risky. Success sparks delight. Failure invites despair. The community, the church, and our obsessed society doubts that passion is a delightful experience. The joys of love spills over to add sparkle to everything else in life. The failure to acquire or to sustain love is a painful experience. (J.A. Lee. *The Colors of Love*, pp. 3-19)

Adultery brings humiliation. It is a slap in the face. The gift of your body and spirit is not cherished. For that brief pleasure, the adulterous spouse is feeling rejection. Exiled from her life, you have been replaced. Betrayed for a meaningless mess of pottage is humiliating. The confusion causes your world to disappear. A man may visualize that all women can be seducers when given the opportunity. Scores of people seek professional help. Now is the time to gather the joy of the Lord as your strength for acts of forgiveness. The sin is shared. Healing love can come. Fault must be confessed as a fault. Perceiving sin is to perceive forgiveness. Sincere repentance is needed as both do something different. Struggling with the human tendencies, repentance alone is the hope of conversion. Joy accompanies forgiveness when it is unexpected and undeserved.

Sin is a prison that one can never completely recover from by themselves. Forgiveness brings back the joy. The couple can be even better. The marriage shall never be the same. That a miracle comes from sinning is a mystery.

A new consuming desire for the other person's love includes forgiveness to everyone involved including the person who got entangled into the frustrating story. Romantic pain feels like physical pain. All have sinned. A person with a forgiving attitude expects sin. They are not superior to the one who has sinned. We tend to rationalize our wrong. A moment of stupidity eclipses an overall record of decency.

Given the amount of sexual adultery everywhere, we wonder about hope for any relationship. Cheating is incredibly common. A majority of your church members have been sexually or emotionally involved with someone outside the marital relationship. In our day, technology, universal hacking into computers, and social media exposes the realities of what is happening.

Accept that adultery can happen. More couples are overcoming affairs when they occur. Adultery is no longer a deal breaker in a relationship. More than 80 per cent of marriages stay together despite the situation. Strong couples make it through infidelity. Most do not.

Adultery for many is the only means they can think of to satisfy their craving for sexual adventure. A sudden blaze of passionate turns existence upside down is called an adventure. Seduced by a capricious woman causes a man to do mad things in the in toxification for adventure. Often, the woman is called an adventuress. The woman mistress boasts that she has miraculously caused her lover to feel thirty years younger.

If your spouse has cheated, it is possible to stay together. God can enable you to pick up the pieces and move on. It is easy for those who have not experienced cheating to see it as black and white. Life gets messy. Emotions explode. People ignorantly believe that "once a cheater, always a cheater."

Cheating is more complicated. Even if a spouse has stated that cheating will not be tolerated adds to the confusion. The healthy healing way is taking time to process the information. Make no decisions about the unwanted event right away. There must be a million little things involved in cheating. Some are an unplanned one-time only encounters wit a stranger. Some just hook up with a colleague at an out-of-town conference. It usually involves someone you know. Not all cheating is the same. Despite modern ethical concepts, cheating spells the end of a marital coupling. Think and pray about it. Does sex with the one person with whom you will be having sex with for the rest of your life really appeal to you now? If you do not want your relationship to be monogamous, get out of the relationship.

Healing of the soul can happen. You can understand the why. This work will enable you to make behavioral changes to ensure that it does not happen again. If either spouse is open to staying in the relationship and working on it together, communicate your desires. Relationships are damaged. Hang in there. If it remains one-sided, nothing will work.

If your relationship was healthy at one point in time, review what made it work. Laurel and I have both seen total healing and a freshness to the relationship. Discuss the positive and negative aspects of the human affair between two children of God. When the unfaithful partner struggles with the real facts, they clearly are still unable to accept the truth which minimizes the motivation for rebuilding. Some relationship therapists specialize in infidelity. This is not the end of your world. Beginning again might bring more joy that you can imagine right now.

Love plows open the hard crust of reality. How mysterious for reminding each other of the incompleteness. Perhaps we come to be aware that we have been sleepwalking through life. Love wakes us up as we desperately desire an eternal union with another. Dignity is not part of love. Dignity can kill love.

During an anniversary we realize that if we are not deeper in love next year, we have failed.

Joy is not found in merely satisfying desires, but in changing your desires so you can choose better desires.

Unacceptable behavior is never the intention when we promise to cling to one another. Bad habits ooze into a relationship until they are out of control. Any sane person with the right mate with whom to share the whole of life must steer clear of anyone who will take selfish advantage. Indications of personal character and emotional strength prevent a stable marriage. Joy comes to those who have good images of themselves. Immaturity and insecurity lead to deviant behavior and love's demise. The most promising place to run is into the arms of a promising lover. Escaping responsibility and commitment is not a human need for love or sex. Normal people do get involved in extramarital relations.

Successful couples find a quiet place where two souls meet before a third person, namely Jesus. Barriers drop. Irritations forgotten. Sins forgiven. Soft mist fills the air. Excitement explodes. What a friend we have in Jesus. Read Matthew 18:20. Comfort comes as relationship skills are built. Couples affirm each other. Both are married to Jesus. Jesus' love is a gracious acceptance, a sacrificial love, an open communication, and full forgiveness distinguish what Jesus exemplified.

With half of all marriages ending in divorce, undeniable evidence proves that we need a strong cohesive love to keep a marriage together. Those cohesive things hold atoms and the whole universe together. God is a mysterious force. We do not understand the impersonal words we use. We find it difficult to commit to a living God. Read Colossians 1:15-17. Jesus makes creation into a cosmos instead of a chaos. The love of Jesus is necessary for a joy-filled marriage relationship. Two finite humans can never hold a marriage together without Jesus the Christ. Jesus told us, "Without me, you can do nothing." Read John 15:15.

Choosing a mate requires asking God to help guide each person. The mystery is that God at this moment where the person is that you will marry. God knows all about both of you. God knows the past, present, and future. That selected person will help you the most. She or he will hinder you the least. Joy and compatibility results. We are not puppets on strings. God gives us free will out of love. Alone, you will probably make a mistake, miss the mark. God's guidance will be an ounce of prevention from error and harm.

Choosing Christ is choosing life, purpose, and meaning. We receive blessings and the joy of heaven. Center your home and life around Jesus. That is the sure road to heaven. The way to heaven is by your personal commitment to Jesus. He forgives all sins. He cleanses us. He lives inside our lives. Jesus is a man. He is more than a man.

God is sexy. Sex is the mystery of a thin line between satisfying spirituality in sex and its distortion. Manipulative relationships between two horny people who are not married is tainted.

That relationship thrives on lies and secrets. Human free will contributes to the eventual pain and embarrassment. When sexuality becomes warped, unintended suffering explodes in every direction. Please do not jeopardize the journey.

Going to bed together and not too late brings oneness. Otherwise, there comes a slow drift of living separate lives. The bedroom is a sanctuary for the two of you. When Laurel and I hear or see 11:11, we usually smile. The mysterious secret known only to us is that when the clock hit 11:11, it was an incredible time when we climaxed after passionate sex.

While you and your spouse are getting undressed, taking off the makeup, showering and brushing teeth, share the joy.

Oneness begins as both enjoy foreplay before you go to your bedroom. Little text messages. Pats on the body. Notes in the other's pocket. The quality of the bedroom routine of a married couple is an indicator of the quality of the relationship.

Sex fits well into the plan of God. To be godly is to be sexy. I firmly believe that the church needs to take back the gift of sex. Allow God to redeem it. Inform us trough the Word. The purpose of this book is not to bring explicit and exact suggestions to how you can do sexuality.

Encourage enjoyment. Unlock the pleasure. Encourage us to wait for it. Ask God to bless it. Multiply the joy. Identify authentic sexual intimacy. Keep sex alive. Enjoy the connection. Keep the marriage glowing. Inhibition and modesty take away from sex. We can maintain discretion in how we dress and carry ourselves. Laurel and I wholeheartedly believe in sex. We work to know sex more bonding, enjoyable, and intimate. Sexual pleasure matters.

If you struggle with not enjoying sex, figure out why. Commit together to be intimate and enriching for both of you. Sex is not just good for your marriage. It is so good for you personally. Sex is a beautiful way to bring babies into the world. God did indeed say go forth and multiply. Sex is how we do that.

Tender soul-drenching sexual pleasure is a marital benefit. Couples think positively about the potential for sex to enrich their lives. When sex fails to communicate love, it is a threat to marital love. Reading the New Testament gives little counsel and guidance on sex within marriage. Grace is the major theme, not sexual joy. Love between "the times" is more enlightening than "how many times." Providing love end joy for each other is unbelievable experience. Sex is most enjoyable in an atmosphere of committee love. Look beyond the bodily delights into the soul of your partner. Feeling oneness brings a spirituality that is sacramental.

Not every time we do sex results in a rapture. Sex is inextricably linked with the way we give and receive love. Women have only recently begun to share with each other what sex really is in terms of their unique experience. (Sheila Kitzinger, *Women's Experience of Sex*, p. 33)

Falling in love means sexual longings and sexual relations. All the acts a couple perform together are the equivalent of intercourse. Going to a movie. Visiting an art gallery. Enjoying a meal. Browsing through a bookstore. These are where we make love. God has created us so that all life is eroticized, not merely the moments in each other's bodies. Being one flesh is not so much about conforming yourself to your partner. Sex is corrupted by the world. The church ignores it. Sex is the ultimate expression of intimacy. Each other's body is an extension of the other's body.

During our acute times of joy, sex is a wonderful experience. If love is illusory, it imitates madness. If a lover is sexually limited, we need to stop deluding ourselves about the sexual abilities. Joy is not something we can live in illusion or fantasy. Given free will, we may be careless in our attachments. Consummating a marriage reassures of our bonds. We need not fear loss. Love has precipitated a larger relationship where affection increases. People are capable of creating the marriage of their dreams. Accepting the grand illusions will not return, keep loving. They need not retell the fairy tale. The dreams are now labeled as puppy love. Illusions must be channeled elsewhere. Desire or the wish to enjoy passionate sex and the physical response to tat wish, can be separated. They might not put them together again. Desire is an intellectual state. We say, "I want to have sex." We mean, "I like the idea of erotic relations." More specifically, I want to enjoy sex with Laurel. Excitement or enthusiasm refers to physical pleasure thoughts. Tenderness. Lust. Joy. Athletic vigor. Excitement happens.

Diminished pleasure is pleasant enough to seek and enjoy. We are bound for better or worse. Much of life is worse. To know joy in marriage, couples must verbalize the difficulties, the hurts, and the disappointments to fully recognize their existence. As conflicts are resolved, sex will become trusting and loving again.

You are all given a new beginning. There will come a time when joy explodes again. Grace offers forgiveness for any sin. Lying. Putting other gods before

God. Making idols. Misusing the name of God. Dishonoring the sabbath. Dishonoring your parents. Murdering another. Stealing. Coveting. Sexualizing sins. If we committed one sin, we have committed all sin against the love of God.

Did you see Forest Gump? Forest was in love with his high school sweetheart. Jenny had passionate affairs with other men. One day, after she became sick, she visited Forest. They enjoyed sex together. Forest had asked her to marry him. She did not want to commit to him.

Can we forget that line in the movie? Forest says, "Jenny, I might not be a smart man, but I know what love is."

Out of their sexual intimacy came a beautiful healthy boy. After Jenny died, Forest raised his son. God makes good out of evil. All human beings can rediscover the joy of the Lord. Why is sexual sin so different in God's eyes than any other?

Renewed hope is around the corner. God is the author of joy. We come to understand how sin causes us loss of joy. Getting it back is not only possible. It will better than ever. Sin sours our attitude. God will give back our spark for living. In our deep connection to the love of God, we rediscover joy.

The New Testament Book of James says, "Count it all joy." Paul gave us unexpected encouragement. Read I Thessalonians 5:16-18.

There is one who understands. As we struggle to be understood we can depend on the compassionate understanding trough love. Please understand me is what Jesus came to communicate the things human being cannot understand. We share an opportunity to experience that voice of love because God first understood and loved us.

We start with a basic kind of understanding. Before we can love one another, we must love others as God loves us. Some couples deny God's love for them. Not accepting divine love is one thing, but not able to allow unconditional love to flow within us and through us misses the mark as denial.

We were created to accept God's love. We need to open our hearts to God. Let allow the Creator pour love inside of you. Go out into the world knowing the lover we were designed to become.

Understanding of spirituality begins with the fact that God loves you. All your duties and abilities were given to you. One appropriate phrase I share with couples is "What you are is God's gift to you. What you become is your gift to God."

It is not too complex for us to understand. Our relationship to God impacts our self-esteem and the way we come to an understanding of our true selves. Complexities entrap us if we let them. Misunderstandings bring distraction. Be assured that this earth belongs to God. We are not to try to flee from it. We are to be the salt, the light, and the yeast. We are to be in it, but not of it. Our inner dispositions shed light on our misunderstandings in our thoughts, our attitudes, and disposition. God 's Spirit is always with us as we receive a clearer perception.

Our questions need to be answered by a Higher Being who knows why we cannot understand.

Couples need a quiet place to rest, pray, and listen. Please understand the divine arbiter. We must say "no" to the world's kind of guidance with a clear conscience. Decide for yourselves what God wants from us. Everything will fall into place. Eureka, you found it. We have so many things to understand with our complex feelings, pressure, and guilt God's strength will enable us to understand our priorities. Be willing to permit God to be in control. Silence alone is all the response we need when we understand and have decided for God. Do not look for a reason, simply do it. When you understand the divine ruler wants you to do something, just do it. Our Lord is not accountable to us. Trust. We don't have to understand the future.

No matter how distasteful it is. No matter how we think it is unreasonable, do it anyway. Couples need to rise on their feet, accept forgiveness, refocus, and start anew. Focus on the Kingdom of God. Seek righteousness. Read Matthew 6:33. The Christian life must never be based on what others say and think.

Meaningful spiritual acts, our covenants, our vows take place first with our understanding within.

Jesus taught us to practice and to model an inner life consistent with its external expression. Understanding and doing a spiritual discipline grip our souls.

A mature pastor who has enjoyed her adventure in marriage told a hurting woman, "Life flies by. Now make your own adventure. Nobody will make it for you." Her happy marriage included a balance of merger and separation.

Couples bring a long list of expectations. Hurt, anger, fear, myth, fantasy, or misinformation create dissatisfaction. Expectations set up disappointment. The expectations gap needs a bridge.

Identify unmet expectations about intimacy. Granting just one wish (expectation) can do wonders. It takes two to maintain a problem. Old habits die hard.

The future in your marital adventure is in your hands. The marriage adventure is moving through. It never remains the same. To know and fully accept this truth releases us from the bondage to the impossible task of attempting to fix it up, once and for all. We can change what is not working. This is possible to function at an amazing level. Many couples have emerged from the childlike helplessness and self-sacrifice that we experienced in much recent marriage and family therapy. Couples can create what theirs can uniquely become.

As couples depend on a new way, they become models for other marriages. Modern couples are the architects for the marriage adventures in the future. Couples long for connection no matter what a wreck their marriage has been. It is like the desire for oneness with God as they understand the divine. We are optimistic that positive changes in marriage will affect all relationships setting change in motion. Unlike the 1975-1985 way of the therapy's counsel, "just get a divorce," people are more accepting instead of rejecting, being responsible not dependent, free to choose not mere sacrifice, love and joy instead of domination. Each goal that is achieved will be a lit candle that combined with supportive other couples could enlighten the world. That is what a ministry of joy to the world means. Like the ripples in a pond, your efforts will affect changes in methods in places we never dreamed possible.

Chapter Four

FINANCING THE JOURNEY

Marriage is an amazing gift of God. We live in a fallen world. Marriage can be weighted down with heavy pressures, especially those that relate to money. Money and accumulating stuff hinder the relationship. More arguments concern money issues than most anything else.

The best novel I have ever read was *The Zacchaeus Solution* written by my friend John Killinger.

Let me share some words from a character in his book. "This, my friends, is what real giving is all about. It is about providing the things ordinary people need. In our case, it is about giving food and shelter, and medicine and love and tenderness, things none of us wants to be without.

"You have been doing this for almost a year now. And every time you have given something to anyone, even a cup of water, you have in effect been giving it to Jesus. It's that simple. You have acknowledged the Lord Jesus wit your gifts as surely as those wise men did when they came to the stable where he was born, and the shepherds in Anthony van Dyck's painting.

"And when we get to heaven, my friends, I know what Jesus is going to say to you. He's going to say, 'well done, good and faithful servants You have been faithful over a few things. Now I am going to make you master over many.'" (John Killinger, *The Zacchaeus Solution*, p. 220)

Money issues begin with a wrong view of the relationship. Read II Timothy 3:16-17. Some keeps their stuff and money separate. God's way is for the two to unite in oneness. One person is not to dominate another. Read I Corinthians 1:10. Part of the work in marriage is to find ways of agreement. It does take time to build unity in marriage. Get to know each other. Handle money together. Talk. Face to face. Compromise is needed. Do something different.

The world has become complex. Thousands of pieces of information are required to be dwelt with by a united couple. We work to survive. Millions live from paycheck to paycheck. No wonder couples get so stressed out. Emotions alone cannot help.

Keep a continuous record of your income and expenses. Live within a budget. Make a plan to pay off your debts. Plan for those unexpected future expenses. Rather than writing more pages about money management, I'll try to summarize the best I have read and reflected on. Our first step is prayer. All our wealth belongs to God. Wise couples set goals. Goals are determined in time frames. Determining your net worth by listing all your assets against your debts. Determine your net income. Federal taxes and property taxes make it difficult. Determine your expenses. Evaluate your expenses against your income. Balance these two factors. Set your priorities. Limited resources will not permit unlimited goals. These reasonable suggestions require communication with discipline. The ultimate attitude toward discipline is realizing it is for our growth.

Happiness is found in most every marriage at first. Laurel and I enjoyed our honeymoon in the Great Smokey Mountains. Starting a lifetime journey, you travel together. That trip involves tunnels, curves, bridges, steep hills, and sidetracks to consider. The requirements are tough.

It is natural to want what others have. Read Exodus 20:17. Couples get all the stuff they can.

Our resources do not come into consideration. Couples need to be content. Read I Timothy 6:6-10.

Money problems are next in line after communication and sex. The responsibility of any marriage is to have a dependable amount of money. Your career or calling, your time, and your energy are symbolized by money. We give our services and talents, our help, our crops, our goods, and pleasure and entertainment so we can have an adequate flow of money. Nobody can live on love. You and your partner need to know each one's attitude toward money. Observe the actual practice of money management. Some are free and easy. Some miserly. Some are ultra-conservative. Disagreements over money derail relationships.

Carelessness, dishonesty, deception, cheating, theft, impulse buying, and selfishness will undermine the financial foundation. Money brings on all kinds of evil. Love of money destroys the home. Money is no small factor. Both people assume roles as adults. Strong marriages require treating one another with dignity and respect.

After marriage, some begin with perks in the beginning. Finances are not a concern. Both become one as people who are financially secure. They have a nice home. Their town has low crime. Laurel is a gourmet cook. There is no drama with in-laws.

All perks and bonus features men nothing if a man or woman dares not paying close attention to the essentials. We jeopardize the journey. We look past the closeness that is crucial to a marriage. Failure comes in marriages where intimacy is optional. Money is so important to some that they will marry a person who is old and rich. The old one just has a young, sexy, gorgeous trophy.

A carefully made budget reflects the goals, hopes, and dreams for the future. Both must submit ideas and input. Don't forget about savings. Each will feel good about having person money.

This money requires no accountability. Freedom, personhood, individuality, and pride in adulthood. I shall say this again and again. Facing fears about money management, love finds the best way.

Nurturing your love through money means the language of giving gifts. Give time and energy to your money. Ignoring money or making it the center of your life are two big errors. Nothing has more symbolic meaning than money. Managing your money gives growth and understanding.

Mismanagement gives confusion, heartbreak or chaos. Cultivate a conscious relationship to money together. Resistance to learning about money is about fear. Stay supportive and gentle. Stop if it gets too intense. A painful schism ignites if we deny how important money is. Balance results with respect for money. God will help you transform financial drudgery into nurture with changes in attitude. Paying mortgage is doing love. You are creating a physical haven, a harbinger of your home in heaven. Reframe your feelings into acts of love.

Trust each other. Experience the dealing with the fears and joys. There is no correct way to deal with money. Some pool everything. Some keep money separate. Nothing is more tragic for your love, your beloved, and yourself than to miss the joys of this life because you kept your eye on the horizon instead of the people you love that surround you. Make managing money fun. Money equals our energy.

There is more joy in the marital partnership if each has a personal account. Every couple should have a joint account at their bank to pay needed monthly bills. Trust is vital to a marriage. Be trustworthy.

Fairness, love, and equality must be stressed in the division of spending money. Money enables

The becoming one flesh, growing together in oneness. Money can be a wedge driving couples apart. Money has been called a coined personality. All living is reduced to dollars. Read I Timothy 6:9-10.

Love of money makes for greediness. Money is a false god to when we destroy ourselves and those we love. Money redeemed in faith is a useful servant. Misusing money or credit causes chaos in the home. Communication and loving negotiation are keys. During our pre-marital workshops, Laurel and I find engaged couples are completely unaware of potential differences in the use of money. These stories show money plays a critical role in the happiness and joys of a marital relationship.

Talking over finances and decisions concerning money prevents an explosion. Laurel and I try to sleep over a decision to prevent impulsive, hasty, and unwise financial decisions. Routine spending comes out of a joint account.

The phrase, please understand me, includes the critical understanding where each is coming from becomes extremely important. Negotiate with each other. Keep the communication channels open.

No matter how much money we earn, we will never have enough to cover all our wants. Huge incomes bring greater desires. Putting God first makes God, not money, the master. Read Matthew 6:33.

Remember marriage is lived as a team. God created us to work together. Marital joy combines individual perspectives. We respect each other's strengths. God helps us in ways we cannot imagine. Impossible goals will be achieved.

Becoming broke after marriage needs better management of finances. To avoid a financial disaster, recover quickly. Do something different. Both people need to get on board. The communication may go poorly. We must work with each other as a team.

There is a difference between the submission we give to God and the submission we vow to another person. We submit to God because God is perfect. Submission to another person is because your mate is not perfect. We need the humble teamwork of our human oneness. Marriage has been ordained as the place where we curb our own freedoms if they prove offensive. Read I Corinthians 8:9, 10:32. Who wins any financial battle of personal whims and wills is not the point. Each individual surrenders as much as possible for the sake of the marriage. Love is honored and built stronger that way. Using "rightness" to dominate becomes "wrongness" no matter how right it might be. Marriages are made for love as a sweet surrender. Willfulness rules in place of sacrifice if we do not "submit to each other in love."

Every successful marriage begins with mutual respect. Never manage the distribution by yourself. Otherwise, we disrespect our life partner. Autonomy is not the way of oneness. Living in this demanding world alone, remember being one means your spouse is your teammate.

We give ourselves into the hands of someone entirely different from the other. We submit in the most loving and reasonable use of the word. God calls both of use to share and to cooperate in mysterious ways that give the impression that there is nothing opposite about the two teammates.

Both hold on to a quiet inner confidence that the relationship itself will help even out the difference of how we manage money. That mystery is not misplaced as couples begin the process of understanding each other as they become more and more like each other. That's because they are more and more becoming like Christ in their particular love. God's desire is for both persons to live in God's likeness. In God's family we become utterly like each other. God is marriage. God is love.

Wrong attitudes toward money fools us and plunges us into serious trouble. Money matters. Understanding money matters begins wit seeing how finances are linked to our relationship.

Relationships are tied to finances. Some are impulsive. Some desire to be like others. It is disastrous to try to relate comfortably with a snow pile of heavy debts. Couples in an effective relationship help each other to control spending.

Financial strength means that we recognize and respect our differences. We realize that opposites attract. Attraction to each other started because bot recognized something that was lacking. Combine these differences into a single plan of action. The amazing headway on your joint goals.

Laurel admits that she is a spender. I am a saver. With love we sometimes interfere with our individual goals. Marriage reduces all decisions to one. Together we decide the choices about money management. Nothing is more particular or far-reaching or even catastrophic than initial and ongoing decision to invite one other person to interfere in the life journey.

Obsessed with nickels and dimes, I have experienced miracles with little amounts of money. My spouse has learned to check with me before making a major purchase.

The bottom line in this life task of using money is to be a tight team. Leaning into each other's strength, we become stable and peaceful. Dream big dreams together and refuse to let go. "The joy of the Lord is your strength." Embrace this truth that you are stronger together.

Jesus said more about money than any other topic. Of his 30 parables, 19 have an economic context. Jesus talked about the rich fool, the lost coin, the spent life of the prodigal, the talents.

There are thousands of scriptures about financial issues.

Money management with all its pitfalls is a must talk about conversation. The Word of God gives your marriage principles. Contentment. Generosity. Simplicity. Joy. Emergency funds. Long-range savings. Financing a marriage includes all of these accomplished in your oneness. You are responsible to put God first. Read II Corinthians 9:6-7.

Prepare a spending plan. Track all your expenses. Together, tell your money what you want it to do to finance your marriage as part of living in the kingdom of God. Read Proverbs 27:23-24.

Simplify your life. Live below your means. Discipline is critical. Read Matthew 6:19-33.

Use time well. Saving money is one of the ways of wisdom in financing a marriage. Three of the kinds of savings that are vital to a successful team are those emergency savings, savings for wants and needs, and retirement savings. Put as much as you can into retirement. You will need it. Read Luke 14:28.

Establish an emergency fund. That might be part of your joint account. If an appliance goes out, the car breaks down, or an illness inevitably comes.

Without emergency funds living becomes more difficult. It's not will we experience emergencies, but when. Read I Timothy 6:9-12.

Pay off any credit card debt. I use Discover for travel and other items needed. Use cash or debit cards for buying things. We would spend less money if we all had to pay cash. Business would be forced to demand so much if we brought cash. A collection of printed money gives a clear picture of how much you are really spending. Our parents and grandparents had no credit cards. They brought enough cash to pay what they needed. Read Luke 14:28.

Preaching and teaching based on the passages of scripture listed above has brought joy and salvation to many of those who heard me share them.

The availability, control, and use of money is a potent form of power. Money is a source of problems. There is just not enough to oil the family system in a proper way. I am reminded of the story about a man who is walking through a jungle. He sees a crocodile near his feet. He climbs up the nearest tree. When he begins to feel safe, he notices a tiger overhead. Just at that moment, he notices a lush strawberry. This old tale is a metaphor for the challenges, struggles, lacking, and just enough strawberries to make it worthwhile.

Look at the choices we can make with our money. We can place that money into a bank fund that brings interest. We could invest in stocks. We could invest in a downward sloop. We could give it away in causes that God would approve. Money can be a means of a legacy. The inevitable conclusion of our earthly living ushers forth what we will leave behind. As we age and our resources dwindle, this issue matters more and more.

The task of marriage is to create a resource with inter-personal enactments that meets or matches needs. The family then grows itself. Marriage creates a new family system. Both spouses want passionate love, and privacy in times they are together. Problems happen when one partner has achieved satisfaction from a career. The other one is still taking on challenges and striving for fulfillment. Unspoken assumptions and expectations of both spouses played out after the marriage leads to conflict. The control of money is an example. It comes as each prepares a will.

Money struggles bring out the worst in marriage. They are motivated by reality. Anger. Revenge. Humiliation. Avarice. Territoriality. Guilt. Lower living standards. Unfair obligations. That's the reality in dealing with money. One of the biggest difficulties is to lesson the impact of the symbolic meaning of money. The amount of money earned may not be enough. To begin to face this financial problem after and not before the marriage union is extremely difficult. Some feel that they have been deceived. No logic or reason can ease the tension, stress, and conflict.

Financing a marriage is about stability. Rising prices. Greed. Lack of control. Inflation. Most are overwhelmed. Laurel and eat yoghurt. We eat it with fruit or homemade stuff. Our eating at home and not out helps in our survival. We cook our own meals. Rarely do we order a pizza or something else. Some make their own yoghurt and granola.

Inviting friends or family to your home to cook meals together brings a special delight. Buying ingredients together in bulk is a great idea. Laurel grows her own herbs. In a wood box on our back porch, we can grow herbs in pots. Basil. Rosemary. Thyme. Mint. Oregano. Experiment with your favorites.

Stability involves compromise. Laurel has always had more expensive tastes than I do. We do try to shop at outlet malls or other wholesale places where we can snag name brands at affordable prices.

Your lifestyle must line up with your actual income, not what you think it is. Too many couples fall down the old rabbit hole.

Accept that everybody's mindset is different. Opposites often attract. They balance each other. One has survived life by being a careful saver. The other one is inclined to spend. These differences can cause marriage issues. This is a communication problem. One partner does not hear the other person's input.

One could just simply bow out from handling the finances. It is dangerous to keep all the money issues to oneself. Remember you vowed to be on the same team. Use your differences to become stronger.

Couples can let salary differences come between them. Laurel had a long career as a registered nurse. The medical field is much more lucrative than a career in church ministry. She also owns acres of farmland. Rarely will two people make the same salary.

My medical physician brother and his spouse, who is a lawyer, make about the same incomes. They tell me that they see "the pot" as our money. Some hold leverages over the other spouse thanks to extra digits on the paycheck. Second marriages tend to think that it's mine and yours. It is not ours.

You both should have equal say in your money and marriage issues. Being committed to your spouse is violated not by an affair, but unfaithfulness to a shared goal. Some feed credit cards that the spouse knows nothing about. Be honest and open. Clear the air. Recommit to your shared goals. We are in this together.

When it comes to money and marriage, unmet expectations cause conflict. People feel dissatisfied and unfulfilled with their spouse when one or the other expect financial matters to go a certain way.

Some think that they must immediately buy a house after getting married. Some feels let down when they celebrate an anniversary in a small apartment. I have purchased more houses than automobiles during my lifetime. Unrealistic expectations pave the way to money and marriage problems.

Clergy are expected to live in a church-owned parsonage. Some never can buy a home. Get your finances in order now so that later together you can make your dreams come true.

Money and marriage go hand in hand. These money mistakes keep us in a bind. Communication concerning money helps to create a life you love and enjoy together.

Ministers I have known and loved continued a downward financial sloop. Financial entanglements strangle their marriage and their very life. There is no pressure like money pressure. When I was a boy, I thought was calling poor people more than rich ones into ministry.
Keep them poor and they'll be humble.

John Killinger ends his novel with a communion service with a minister and his wife and his congregation. "Myralee, the body and blood of Jesus Christ, given for you," the husband whispered.

"I love you darling," she responded.

At that sacred moment, he realized all over again . . . more deeply than ever before . . .what a rich life he enjoyed as a minister of the gospel.

Chapter Five

COMMITMENT TO IMPOSSIBLE PROMISES

Marriage vows cannot be contemplated without the love and grace of God. Keeping impossible promises, we affirm that we will care for each even 50 years from the wedding day. A couple will shake their heads in wonder. They are amazed that they have kept their vows. It will bewilder them to believe what they know is true.

Commitment means making a serious promise to each other in front of family and friends. We become a team. We navigate through life together. We commit to support, to love, and to encourage each other wherever the adventure takes us. The last nearly four decades have brought incredible memories. Despite all our flaws we would choose each other again.

When the river is too wide, the hill seems too steep, the mountain looks too high, God is there.

God spoke the earth into being. God scattered the stars into place. God split the Red Sea wide open. God works miracles.

Couples do not need to figure anything out. Read Psalm 32:8. This is the secret. Most married people feel overwhelmed. They hold on when they become discouraged. It is not what we have in us. It's about who we have inside us. Nothing is impossible for God. That assurance means nothing is impossible for us.

Conditional and unconditional love. Couples ponder these types of love. As we grow order, our perception of love changes. The less time we have left, the more important real love becomes. That is the reason I am using words that will satisfy your commitments to love each other forever. Unconditional love is the kind of love we give and receive from God and others, including our spouse.

Giving that love is never easy. Sacrifice and selflessness are required. Time and effort from giving love is worth it. Conditional love is simply love with strings attached. Provided if you stay committed to our vows, I will love you.

Otherwise, we will just cut them off. We are done. I'm going to move on. Conditional love manipulates and controls others. We then withhold love and intimacy.

Cleave. Read Matthew 19:5. The word "to cleave" is to be joined, or to cling to. The two will embrace. Cleave is used when speaking of the loyalty that exists between two committed persons. It can mean "socially sanctioned." Cleaving is a divine sanction. It is permanent.

Conditional love gives a distorted image of reality. Unconditional love brings on security, doing what we have promised is in a place where we both belong. It's who we become in our oneness. In Christ we belong to the family of God. Another person's weakness will not cause you to withdraw, your friendship, and your support. Conditional love pulls the rug out from another's feet. That is why commitments and vows become impossible to keep. Unconditional love is the stuff of a radical and daring commitment.

Sometimes couples are confronted with a challenge so impossible that there is no solution.

Your soul is heavy. You can think of nothing you can do. Riding on an emotional rollercoaster, you wonder if anything will ever be done.

Impossibilities are the platforms upon which God does joyfully. My dear readers, I want you to cherish faith. With humans there are many impossible barriers. With God all things are possible.

Audrey Hepburn said, "Nothing is impossible. The very word itself says that I'm possible."

Our beliefs and stubborn wills hold us back. Couples must rebuild their self-limitations to gain a life that is worth living. Others will be inspired to do the same. The extraordinary is the focus. The impossible stays impossible until it is done. Do it.

Who one marries is the most important decision in a life journey. Marriage is like declaring mutual dependence in a revolution. We have lived as one. Becoming two is like an invasion. People who succeed in long, joy-filled marriages are the winners. The impossible promises lure us on.

The vows of marriage and the responsibility of building a Christ-honoring home are treated in a secondary matter. Families are taught by the world by their examples. Ours must be an example to others. Clear direction from each other and the Bible if our home is what God wants it to be. Staying married brings encouragement. We have made a vow to God. Every married couple made a promise in a pledge before God. If God cannot trust me to keep my vows, there is no trust for doing anything else.

This sounds harsh. We do make mistakes that God may heal. The love of God is greater than any of our failures. Falling is not staying down. Only by being trusted and trustworthy can couples build a lasting marriage. The joy of the Lord brings with it our trustworthiness. Total commitment needs God's strength. That is how marriages overcome the impossible. Without that strength, we can't get along. One or both may not like themselves. They are looking for somebody to give them a reason for being. Insecurity and not knowing who they are with no confidence in self-worth. They do not love themselves, so they cannot love the person they live with. Some spouses do know themselves. They want love and they desire to give love. The other is already looking elsewhere. Read I John 4:20. No outsider will be able to enter. One flesh cannot be divided. a fenced enclosure that two have built together. A married couple is one flesh. One flesh cannot be divided. We have a responsibility before. God for our families. Read Acts 16:31. Before God, my faith involves my family. I am responsible.

Life is vast and complex. Temptations and pressures come from so many places and situations. Our home base is important. During my ministry, I have traveled to many places. No matter where I am, no matter which continent or how many miles from home. Emotionally, I am home. My heart is focused on my heavenly home. In the vastness of life, like the vastness of the globe, my focal point is home. God knows about that. God gives us our home now and our final home. The temporal and the eternal join in our souls. Live with family love around you now. Home is a harbinger of eternity.

Think of the impact if married couples would give a visible testimony to the love in their marriage because God is love. People of the world do not realize that it is possible to receive the love from God, because they cannot see God in overflowing love, especially in marriage. This influences generations. Faithfulness to our spouse gives a legacy to our children. The home is the framework in which our children try their wings. They need to know their parents live a commitment that is not shifting. They need solid footing. They pass the love to the next generations.

We learn to pray in the home. They learn marriage in the workshop held at home. Experiencing human love, they accept divine love. Family duty connects with joy. When spouses fulfill their duty to each other, they fulfill duty to their children. Joy comes.

Passion peaks when we are young. Marriage peaks during old age. The passion never wanes. A mysterious magic is felt during all seasons. We must burn the ships behind us as we risk this journey. Marriage is not a settling down. It is a faithful revolution two people take on together. Couples need to be aware of the crisis nature in marriage.

They must find joy in each other's successes. The mystery unveils how we correct each other's vices. The hope is to enjoy the deepest steady joyful moments in each step in the journey.

Marriage begins with the vows. When we make clear promises, we are committing to be faithful. A new third thing, the relationship has started. It is a new enduring trust. Promises made. Promises heard. Promises witnessed. Promises heard. Promises remembered. Commitment
Is the sure foundation for eternal joy. We have done what God has done. We make a covenant of love. That covenant creates a oneness that matures us against any storm that blows our way.

Think about the meaning of your vows. We commit "for better or worse, in plenty and in want, in joy and in sorrow, in sickness and in health, as long as we both shall live." With "God and these witness" we express our commitment. The quality and longevity of our marriage depends on it.

George Muller said, "Faith does not operate in the realm of the possible. There is no glory for God in that which is humanly possible. Faith begins where human power ends." No matter how tough the things you encounter, stand firm. Do not fear. Go forward. Read Isaiah 58:11, Second Samuel 22:33, Philippians 4:6, and Zechariah 9:12. Read these passages with believing optimism. Those impossibilities that confront us become God's opportunities to show "the joy of the Lord is our strength."

Trust God even if things you are facing make no sense. Seek God in prayer as you read those selected passages listed in the last paragraph.

An encouraging friend asked Laurel and I why we love our children and family so diligently.

He replied, "Because they are ours." God would say the same in the divine love for you. Because of that love, we can be confident about the future.

Expect to be surprised by what gifts God will give you. Visualize God going before you. See God standing behind you. Experience God's guidance. Joy and miracles are bound to happen. God will create a way where there is no way.

God specializes in changing impossible situations. God moves in mystery. Muhammad Ali used to say, "The man who has no imagination, has no wings."

Marriage turns "I" into "we." It is give and take. It is enjoying each other's company. Unconditional love seeks to give and not take. Put each other first. Hold no conditions.

Impossible solutions come in our imaginations. When Laurel and I were dating, we began to picture what it might be like to be married to each other. Before we built our new home in Elmwood, we imagined what would become possible.

By now you know, I enjoy basketball. In the season of 1974, UCLA held an eighty-eight-game winning streak. Despite the overwhelming odds, Notre Dame's coach Digger Phelps helped his team imagine that they could beat the Bruins. He told his players that they needed to believe they could beat the nation's best basketball team.

A week before the game, Phelps asked his team to imagine how beating UCLA would feel. He even led them in a dance to celebrate as if they had just won the game. Phelps persisted every day with creative motivation words and tools. By the last practice, the Fighting Irish needed no more prompting. Those of us who saw the game on television were simply amazed. That last three pointer from the far-left side of the court dropped into the net with a swish heard all around the college basketball world.

My imagination has enabled me to write novels, discover metaphors, and to remember events that bring my words that really give people hope. The noted scientist Albert Einstein said, "Imagination is more important than knowledge. For knowledge is limited to all we now know and understand, while imagination embraces the entire world, and all there ever will be to know and understand."

Commitment is an attitude. A way of thinking. A mindset. Navigating through the still waters and the storms, hope is so important. Barriers such as the cost being more than you thought, more determination that you expected, messier than you anticipated. Self-centeredness. Stubbornness. Emotional baggage. Lack of clarity. Being too busy. Poor communication skills. Barriers fall in a committed marriage. Couples can make it work.

Christ-centered living chooses commitment, not convenience. Marriage is an important commitment. We commit to family. Friends. To our churches. Talk is cheap. Loyalty and faithfulness come with following Jesus. Read Ruth 1:8-17. During the period of the judges, Israel experienced a horrible drought. Life became precarious for Ruth and two widows. Her life tests were many and varied.

Commitment is essential to a successful relationship. The Book of Ruth does not share the adjustments she and Boaz had after the marriage. Ruth vowed to make the people of Boaz's family her own along with his faith in God. Ruth understood what she had committed to by marrying Boaz. They knitted their lives together.

A commitment is a promise made from love. Expecting no return, it is sheer joy. Commitment means to be in turmoil with each other, rather than live alone in tranquility. My promise was made to Laurel and Laurel only. I wrapped my whole life and calling into my covenant with her.

"Faithfulness unto death" is our summons to work while there is life. Those impossible promises are seldom perceived until the marriage has lost its golden sheen.

The marriage vow has obligated both of us. It is God you serve when you serve God's child who is your spouse. This requires total abandonment to your spouse's world and yours that will be changed into a new and better world. This is impossible without the grace and love of God. No marriage can last without the mysterious touch of grace that enables each one to keep improbable promises to each other. These promises are kept 20, 30, 40, 0r 50 years from now. We will shake our heads in wonder. We are amazed that we have kept our word. This is a complete abandonment to the will of God. Only the ignorant marry with the illusion it will be easy. We rally have no idea what we are getting into. Our sacred vow is a mystery. It is a puzzle. Love is not an emotion or an experience. An act of the will. A promise. A resolution. Successful marriages look back at the impossible promises. Those wild vows made before God depends on trusting the divine as the source of renewal and strength.

Scores of couples come to Laurel and I declaring that they are not in love. They are out of love.

Doing something different is a counseling suggestion to return doing what they did when they were "in love." It may mean just sitting with each other on a porch swing. Supernational attraction is the key to renewed attraction. This is action that is required in eternity. The earthly journey is a surface journey seeing the glass darkly. When we live in love face to face with God, we learn to see the invisible and to the impossible. It is the experiencing of eternal life. Marriage teaches us to withdraw from temptation to change partners, to love each other, to be single-minded.

Giving a binding promise is an act of faith. People are not naturally faithful. A public declaration of vows in a church will not automatically transform us into creatures of steadfastness. God makes love possible. Our wedding is proclaiming the power of God with eternal significance. Marriage is to hold a unique bonding. This unique bond is keeping each other going. Bound together, you both can fulfil the dream you otherwise would not have. You would not even attempt to live your dream. Being excited together in the good times and being the encouragement when what you are doing becomes a challenge. This amazing adventure centered on love never grows tired. It is never completed. It finds ways to fully express itself. The mystery of marriage is that it becomes more and more amazing. Treasure your amazing gift. Your little team gets stronger and stronger.

Love must be practiced inside the home before it reaches out. The oneness in marriage is now a priority. Both are united in love to every one of the children of God. If both do not fully love one another first, they are not capable of loving themselves or any other person.

Love is central to the process of marriage, commitment, and mate selection. One of the goals of love acts is marriage. Marriage enforces fidelity and exclusivity. Marriage is a public commitment. It is enforced by kin. Male failures surrounding work and female failures surrounding willingness and ability to bear children are concerns. Love is the conception of offspring during the marriage.

Self-love is authenticity. God's kind of love begins with who you are. It means your willingness to be seen just as you are. Love begins with each individual. All love happens inside of you. Love is felt in your whole person. You take it all in. The depth. The heart. The warming. The vulnerability. The intimacy. Revealing the secrets within lightens the darkest days. You open to the flow of love. Looking within your own soul gives you access to lasting and profound eternal love. The essential thing about self-love is being completely you. Love happens in the moment you give up what you think you should be. Be who you really are.

Virginia Satir wrote "My Declaration of Self-Esteem," which I have used in decades of pastoral psychotherapy, is powerful insight. Part of it reads, "In all the world, there is no one else exactly like me. Everything that comes out of me is authentically mine, because I alone chose it. I own my fantasies, my dreams, my hopes, my fears. I own all my triumphs and successes, all my failures and mistakes." (Virginia Satir, *Peoplemaking*, pp. 250-251)

Self-love is becoming yourself. To be authentic means to be your own author Being my own author, I write my own script. I choose the dialogue. I choose the parts of me that I bring into my story. I play myself in the drama of living. The single most important thing we can do in ministry, in any business, is being yourself. Trust yourself. You make better decisions. You determine what to like about yourself. Human beings become anxious to improve their own circumstance. They are not willing to improve themselves. What other people think of you is really none of your business. Let them have their thoughts. Your thoughts belong to you.

Saint Augustine wisely said, "People travel to wonder at the height of mountains, at the huge waves of the sea, at the long courses of rivers, at the vast compass of the ocean, at the circular motion of the stars. They pass by themselves without wondering."

Being our true selves is not being a conformist. Conformist lead average lives. Perhaps for some, this starts in schools. They are molded to like alike. Those children dress alike. They talk alike. They think alike. We reward them as they reach advance levels of school. They are promoted in the workplace by competing effectively with conformity. A life of mediocrity often follows. Know yourself. Love yourself. Love life. Seek joy.

Love with the love of your life. Nothing worthwhile is easy. Determination is needed. God will guide you. Self-love brings healing from past baggage. Expect great things from God. Attempt great things for God. Love of self makes you aware of how the past affects your present. You no longer solve problems by attacking others. Your mate becomes your priority. Love releases anger and bitterness. Love reboots relationships. All your work toward being loving comes together. Define who you are now. Love increases worth, self-esteem, confidence, and kindness. Love guides you to your ultimate purpose. Love accepts healthy boundaries. Love brings repentance from things that have given guilt and shame.

Rekindle the spark. Visualize a flame. See the colors. Enjoy the warmth. Reminisce. Feel as you did when you first fell in love. Passion was there. Fascination filled you up. Permit the memories to flow. Remember each other's smell. Recall the smile that captivated your heart. Bask in the sense of the aliveness you have created. This is not just a memory. It is your present.

The person facing you in this and every moment s the very one you fell in love with. Allow your admiration and love to flow. If you feel passionate, let these feelings fill you.

Commit yourself to love and the impossible promises turn into loving acceptance and the giving of the best you have been given to give. Committed people care less about any other person to whom to make a commitment. There will be no other love. Love has been willed by God from eternity. Marriage is a spiritual experience. God explodes into our lives with unexpectedness and mysterious transformation. Marriage is a step of faith. A completely new understanding of what love means as a vision from God. This awesome plan changes the entire lives of one another. It may be likened to a religious conversion. Only by loving God can we love each other.

Laurel is a better Christian than I am. When we were committed to marry, we joined Hillcrest Baptist Church together. Laurel grew up as a Methodist. I was serving as minister of family life for the congregation. One of the spiritual practices of a Southern Baptist Church is to be baptized by immersion. Pastor Hawley gave me the honor of baptizing Laurel as a symbol of her being part of that colony of the kingdom of God. Love came bubbling from the water as tears in our eyes reflected her beauty and goodness.

Matrimony is a holy order. Wholeness is part of our commitment. We have chosen not to live as a single adult. By choosing one particular person, we close the possibility of marrying anyone else. Accepting our own imperfection is baffling. Marriage as an act of faith surprises us as we accept the imperfections of another.

Dream back to when you were first wooing each other. In your early married years, you could never get enough of each other. Think of activities you enjoyed. Schedule some new ones to do together now.

Acceptance is present in each exultant love. All people crave it. Love always reaches out to wholeness. Full acceptance is not cheap or easy. It does bring deep healing. We naturally embrace the whole person. Both are mirror images of themselves.

Never try to change your partner. Take responsibility for your own life. We each have an individual perception of the world. Stop wasting energy on changing your partner. Spend that energy on changing yourself.

Behold the unique beauty in your love. There is no other place to be. There is nothing to do but to accept your eternal lover. Feel your soul as it breaks open in devotion, grace, and love.

Now just smile.

Commitment is one thing when we are young and vigorous. We stay committed during the time of our decline. We become bald. Rather than crying over the loss of our youth, both must rejoice in the grace in the face of advancing years. Serious illness causes one or both to be bedridden for the rest of life. Commitment. Permeated. Acquiescence. Continuous giving in. Gracious compliance. These are just part of the struggle with another human being. Commitment is not imposed. Everything about marriage is personalized. There would not be the exact frustrations or disappointments had you married someone else.

Creeping old age is another factor. Age cuts into a person's attractiveness. They become anxious when they lose their alluring glow. Tons of money is spent each year in order to stop beauty from fading. Everything appears tied to appearance. Roughness to the skin. Roundness of the stomach. Sagginess to the cheeks. Floppy body parts. Lack of energy. Weaker bodies. She is vulnerable to any man who tries to prove to her that she has what it takes to attract a lover.

Nobody in the eight billion souls on earth could fit the imagination or life fantasy like the one God chose for you. No compliance is more personal or necessary than that required in commitment to marriage. Love relinquishes control. Love permits God to be in full control.

Love and marriage are not a blind thing. Perfect love remains perfect even if is one-sided. Love is a covenanted relationship. (Lewis Smedes, *Sex for Christians*, pp. 167-197)

Love covers a multitude of sins.

Marvel at the majesty of forgiveness. Mail a love letter to a place where you go together before you both arrive there. Dedicate a song on the radio to your love. Give a gift that leads to more giving. Give your love a bottle of massage oil. Give scented soap. Give some romantic music.

Laurel and I have cherished giving each other messages. She invested in a message table. We lovingly rub each other with massage oil. We completely relax. We forget about everything.
Imagine that.

Initiate a shower together. Wash your lover. Wash every beautiful part.

Unrequested public displays of affection are priceless. Show the world that you love this person. I love it when Laurel does outrageous things. She covers the bed with flower petals.

When I left Nebraska to take a call to lead the Appalachian Counseling Center in Bristol, Tennessee, we missed each other. When Laurel came for a visit, she put on a sexy night gown. She had delicious things to taste. She stirred my imagination with alluring pictures. She played sexy music. She began to kiss me passionately. Her touch was magic. We enjoyed a long sexual connecting.

Now that's love. That's spiritual bonding.

Bonding can include finding a private spot in nature where you can make love without being disturbed. We have made love in our gazebo, on the banks of the Missouri River. You're smiling now. Improvise your own magic. Be creative. When making love, do it your way. Feel the energy moving back and forth. Connect the rhythm of God's creative with the rhythm of your unique love. Cover everything with a soft coating of love.

Our promises do seem impossible. The pressures of life overwhelm us. We are tense and overloaded. We desperately need soul refreshment. We can become lifeless, drained, and dull.
We all have five senses. Each is a channel of awareness. This is the way for renewal and exquisite joy. Senses stimulate sensual selves. Create pleasant smells to celebrate special times. Put fragrant flowers in your home. Communicate to your partner nonsexual ways you would want to be touched.

Every person enjoys and appreciates the magic of a tender touch. Even on a difficult day, you can rub the neck or back. Place your palms on your lover's back. Move in leisurely large circles around the shoulders. Rub the muscles on each side of the spine using your thumbs. Find sensual extras.

Fill your home with colorful balloons. Light candles. Play wild music. Burn musky incense. Get your aliveness juices flowing. Rub the feet. Feet are sensitive. Use some massage oil. Feet contain magic nerve pathways to healing.

Don't wait. Life is a brief time. Let me give you a challenge. See how various people have accomplished the impossible. It is designed to be a fun journey. Enjoy the ride. Imagine your life as a movie with an incredible ending. The greatest movie writers end the story with an unexpected twist.

God has designed eternity to be a thousand times what we could ever imagine. Faith is courage that has said its prayers. Brave getting out of your comfort zone. God gave us courage. Courage is located inside everyone of us. Dare to reach for it. Some sailors once said, "A ship in a harbor is safe, but that is not what ships are for."

Chapter Six

YOU AND I, INCORPORATED

The traditional way when I grew up was my father going off to work each day. My mother stayed home. Mother raise three boys, cleaned the house, handled family arrangements. My father was the breadwinner. In this modern era, the division of labor is less common.

As women entered the workforce, changes have come. A. J. Beaber titled her novel, *You and I, Inc.* Hers is a story of a young woman becoming aware of relationships, realities of sexuality and spirituality. Her husband is a dentist. His income makes him the major breadwinner. She has raised beautiful children. Splitting the household and childcare duties can lead to conflict. Together, they have made joy on the journey.

Even if your partner labors outside the home, they shoulder most household chores. Dividing the work matters. Another key factor is the couple's belief about what is and should be each one's responsibility. Understanding how "you and I, incorporated" works has implications that satisfy a healthier and happier marriage.

In current marriages, equality is a part of the "please understand me" communication. Today more men take on childcare and housework. Still some women perform more than an equal share for creating a happy home. Women tend to plan family time. Women suggest vacations, education events, visits to the zoo, and spontaneous fun things.

Cultural expectations and traditions suggest that women oversee the home. This is especially true for military and missionary families, foreign correspondents, firefighters, police, and the realities of using the gifts, talents, and love for the world.

Home chores are not created equal. Some are mundane. Requiring little effort or challenge, some labor is still designated as women's work. Oneness is affected by inequality. Women suffer consequences in their well-being. Women feel more personal strain. Mothers have an old "second shift" as they work when they come home. Leisure time is compromised.

Dissatisfaction with the division of labor is perceived as unfairness. That hurts the oneness. Married life is less distressed when there is more egalitarianism. We are called to together work with equally to glorify God. Joy in our helping is possible. In the Olympics in Tokyo, we see works of strong talent. Eric Liddell, an Olympic runner said, "When I run, I feel God's pleasure."

Whether you or your partner is doing more than their fair share of housework, the effect is the experience of more negative emotions. My wife and I have similar personality types—INFJ and INFP. Her letters can be summarized as I Never Find Perfection. Mine could read Inner Nuances Foster Journeys. Men and women both find inequality distressing. Men express more negative anger and unhealthy rage in comparison to women.

Both partners live in a society with cultural expectations for how to divide their lives. Most value equality. Both are impacted when expectations are not met. Those who agree that household labor should be divided equally are happier and experience more marital joy.

Until Adam and Eve sinned in the Garden of Eden, the working atmosphere was described as paradise. Work by this couple brought equal joy. Work was fulfilling and rewarding. After breaking the relationship with God work became distasteful and difficult.

The adventure in marriage must include work. Today work is organized, impersonal, rigid, and fractionalized. In workplaces today, the moment a worker is inspired to use initiative in the method of working, the boss would object. The meaning of work should be the satisfaction of the instinct for adventure. The jobs of today are merely a mechanical routine. Most work no longer has the lure of adventure. They keep their weary eyes on the clock.

That was not the end of the story. Jesus came to the world to restore our relationship with God. We will never create a perfect work environment like the Garden. Despite sin, it is possible to make work joyful. Accepting and acting on this truth, we can bring joy into wherever we work.
Work will continue to be an unfair experience and we all will see it as meaningless.

Pastors do well to remember that church leadership requires us to serve the people we lead. Living in intimate relationship with God, we become consistent with God's plan for us. We "enter into the Master's joy."

Consistent beliefs are more important that the communication about beliefs. Effective communication will find mutual grounds. Finding joy in marriage will not make life less busy and demanding. You and I, Incorporated will be stronger. Days will bring more gratitude. Hitting the ground running, we make coffee, we shower, we kiss and continue running all day long.

God's calling in my life is my own. Ministry and all work are exciting, stimulating, and enjoyable for me. My unique place as the Minister of Joy to the World has been the way of helping millions find joy in marriage oneness and in work. My vision is perhaps quixotic, but worth every ounce of my energy. Writing this book celebrates feelings of fulfillment for human relationships. I am grateful for the stories of how joy busted upon their life and work.

Joy is doing mundane tasks together. Turn on the music and work together. Complete the not-as-fun together. Not only will the work go faster, but it will be more fun to spend the time. Each year Laurel and I put up 12 dozen ears of Nebraska corn during hot summer days. This requires buying the best sweet corn, shucking each ear, cleaning the corn completely. We place two boiling water pots on the stove. For three minutes we place four to six ears of corn into the boiling water. As each ear cools, we begin the process of cutting the corn from its cob, and vacuum pack it in plastic bags. It is really hard work, but what joy to eat it all year long.

Whatever the occasion or needed task, we can share celebrating everything in oneness and equality. Enjoying each other's company while you successfully celebrate will keep joy in the center of the marriage. I now have hundreds of pictures in scrapbooks. Viewing the photo books of the marriage journey is a fun way to go back and see how far you have come.

When life gets difficult, we lose sight of the joys. Forever running to work, to our children and grandchildren's events, piano lessons, baseball games, and home again, there appears to be enough time to smell the roses.

To work without God is folly. As we pursue a richer life with togetherness, we must walk closely with God. Do not overlook the tremendous and strong resource at your hand. God is yours to draw upon and share in competing your marriage related work. Be filled with God's caring. In Christ we understand the unqualified and the unending love of God. Love makes it possible for me to forgive those who derided my thoughts. They rejected me and I suffered the pain. Love is the final necessary part to know joy. Whether we see work as drudgery or joy, we treasure our bountiful and abundant life that Jesus promised to give us.

Matthias had work before he was voted to be an apostle. He had been faithful to his regular field of work. There are no surprises with God. We must be ready as were the early followers of Jesus to leave all and follow. They may have had a full-time career s a carpenter, a tax collector, following a new role because that's what God has chosen for us. God chooses us. We are called to a verity of ministries. When we committed our lives to Christ, we made ourselves available. Once God decides how we are to be used, change can alter the plan at any moment. We do not know what tomorrow brings. Turn to God to work out for you the messes that others put you through. Watch what happens when you speak out for the poor, against racism, for reduction of arms or against the consumerism. Expect to be disliked. Watch what happens when you try to do something about the destruction of people by gambling, alcohol and drug abuse.

When a married couple handles needed tasks, each makes full use of their skills. Work becomes much more enjoyable. Joy starts with individual initiative and individual feelings that they are in control. Stress enhances the experience. Still each one needs a certain amount of control over what is happening. Debilitating stress is created out of a feeling of lack of control.

Recreation work is just that, the creation, again. Solutions come even while taking a shower, when we least expect it. Play is the opposite of work. When we work, play is essential. Play relaxes. Play enhances focus. Play engenders a team spirit.

Joy touches our lives in daily work. A surgeon feels the glow of accomplishment as she completes a lifesaving procedure. Intense joy fills a mom as she bathes her child. A young construction engineer stands and brushes sand from his clothing, as he sets out to show his achievement to his mother and father.

God wants to satisfy us. God has unlimited grace to offer. What a friend we have in Jesus!

God and other people have given me their tears, their embrace, their edification, their tenderness, their correction, and their love. In Christ I am free to live. Free to be flexible. Free to move. Free to fail. Free to succeed. I am and I have a precious self. God created that self. It is mine. There is no end to my growth and development here now, and no end when I depart satisfied in divine love, grace, and joy. I am an original creation.

God has me. I am God's glory. Within me, I have promises, character, action, and reputation that belong to God. We gain a matchless joy of belonging. Everything will fit together as we enjoy the eternal family. We need not to fret about what comes and what does not come. Followers of Jesus belong to an eternal plan. We do the work of God, and we live in God's life today or in our eternal home.

Joy consists of being, not having or knowing. Joy brings a warm glow of a person who is at peace. That self-assurance rises from understanding that she is loved just as she is. God's love fills her. She rejoices in the freedom as a child of God to work together in oneness. God became incarnate God and works with us. God never has sat off in the distance and command that we do things. During Jesus' time on earth, we relish his hallmarks of an inner calm and joy. We perceived his inner peace even in death. With the evidence of history and the big changes in his disciples. We move into the future with deliberation and calmness. A joy-filled workplace gives us the freedom to use our talents and skills without being crushed by autocratic bosses or the constant change in our supervisors.

Couples I encounter, regardless of class, income, education, nationality, and race want an opportunity to meet the needs of their families while doing something fun and useful for meeting the needs of the world. The marriage adventure is for life. Marriage is an excellent instrument for the constant renewal of adventure. The adventure of marriage and the adventure of work affect each other. Life is a unity.

God alone can promise things that have never happened in all human history. In joy, we summon the future s we bring the past into the present. We affirm and accept God's trustworthiness. Our future is the assurance of eternity. We start to live in joy now despite the circumstance that surround us.

Men enjoy caring for the lawn. Christian author Gary Chapman invented the term "love languages." Chapman attempts to describe the preferred ways people give and receive love. Without a long discussion of the five love languages which Chapman has done quite well in his many best-selling books. Physical touch, acts of service, gifts, words of affirmation, and quality time. Now that we are both retired, we can enjoy more quality time.

We share a home office. Laurel cooks fantastic meals. It used to be a rare time when we could sit together for a meal. She enjoys her music room. She likes communication with her family. As I view her tremendous love for life, I rejoice. I love her dearly. I want her to have what brings her joy. She feels free to enjoy quality time with her friends.

We crave our relationship the way photographers crave a perfect light. Just as a chef craves the best ingredients, fresh and full of taste, we enjoy more than a shallow relationship. We each have a love language. These are a vital part of the "please understand me" communication. The more we understand the concept of love languages, the better we are equipped to love well and to express how we best receive love.

Love resets the course of our life journey. We realize that love comes from God. Love comes out of the blue. We could neve anticipate how love comes. God explodes into our lives with breathtaking unexpectedness. Love brings sweeping renewal and transformation. To love is to know a revelation from God. Love gives insight into the power and possibilities of life together. Marriage is a mysterious step of faith. Entering the grace of marriage, we slowly grasp love with a whole new meaning. We understand what love really means. It is a God-given vision. One special person causes it to happen. We fully commit to dedicate our lives to the experience, the exploration, testing, renewing, and enjoying the continuous renewal of envisioning love.

Work is a shared task. To share space in the same house is not sharing the labor which maintains the marriage inside the house. Each serves the relationship. Arrogance is assuming the marriage exists to support either one in their chosen work. People shouldn't marry only for that benefit.

Work is survival. The purpose of all laborious duties is for the marriage, for the good of making a home together. The joy and strength of marriage comes out of this interweaving, the sharing of the work for survival. Marital work must come consciously and willingly. Love allows us to give up the selfish power to control. Living and working in humility is harder than being passionate. We accept our inability to control the world.

In "Pippa Passes," Robert Browning wrote:

"All service ranks the same with God—
With God, whose puppets, best and worst,
Are we. There is no last or first."

Cultural habits run deep. Grandparents and parents, and even each partner maintains expectations of what are a wife's tasks and what are those of the husband. Each must comfort each other in the choice to share the common job of survival. Flexibility is vital as the marriage changes to accommodate new necessities. That third thing, the relationship, remains bound to unrealistic restrictions and remains undeveloped. Criticism and guilt must be laid aside. Revision is necessary. No person who has chosen to marry should never feel neglected, dominated, or used. Both work with a complete commitment to the survival tasks.

David Clark, one of my best supervisors at Valley Hope shared a rhyme wit me, "Methods are many, principles are few. Methods change often, principles never do."

Marriage is a union of differences. The Spirit gives different gifts to each for the common good. Celebrate the differences by willingly choosing the work that fits each other. This way permits true personhood. Survival work esteems each individually. Every marriage is different. Freedom and satisfaction follow with joy and continual interest in each one's work.

Each one's spirit travels with each other like an invisible angel, who sees what each does and encourages one another. I am a presence that sustains my wife. When she applied for the vigorous job as director of nursing for the Dialysis Centers in Nebraska, she hesitated. I help with the application. I assured her she could do that important task. Laurel spent 20 years of her nursing career for that corporation.

Faithfulness includes sharing, which was the vow at the beginning. If the two tend to have a life independent of their spouse, the marriage is neglected. Work sharing offers all of one's work in service to the marriage. Both must resist every temptation toward independence, toward personal liberty or toward "doing one's own thing." Couples know best when to take on a particular responsibility. With God and our spouse, we are a team.

Marie Chapian writes about a distraught woman. Her voice is loud. High pitched. Short breaths. Snapped sentence endings. "That husband of mine does nothing around the house. The place could fall apart for all he cares. I am the one who shovels the walk. Mows the lawn. Fixes the light switch. Drags out the garbage. Cooks. Cleans. Chauffeurs the kids."

This woman believes her husband is not fulfilling his obligations "A man is supposed to do the fixing and the muscle work." The husband falls short of her expectations. He is wrong. Back in the days when one person was the breadwinner, husbands were horrified at the idea that a wife wants to go out of the house to work. She says that she will hire a housekeeper to do the laundry and clean the house.

Putting the other under personal expectations means telling myself that others owe it to me to live up to my expectations. Misery-not joy comes out. Life becomes a nightmare network of obligations. (William Backus and Marie Chapian, *Telling Yourself the Truth*, pp. 139-140)

Our ultimate work is to share the love of the life of God. Wen working for God in the world, we ignite a burning fire. The flames consume actions and things that shall not conform to the mysterious exigencies.

Working with God links us with Christ and the work of salvation. We are subject to one another and to God. You and I, inc. is possible within our human limits. Marriage crates an atmosphere where joy and miracles happen. The incorporated goal is to work or play to serve God as each one is called to do. Jesus commanded us to love one another. This love is the same as God has given us. That's the mystery and the joy of oneness. "You and I" incorporate is a communion. This is one of the deepest mysteries of personhood. We are never a single person in a working partnership. Creation and grace work together in the plan of God. Redemption restores what we have corrupted or distorted. We continue the work of creation.

In heaven the work will be completed. We know creation's goodness. Part of the mystery is that love and work will be enhanced and glorified in the perfect heavenly kingdom. Our human need for festivity will be satisfied in the marriage of the Lamb. The witnesses, alive in earth and heaven will support us freely. When in the wedding "in the sight of God and these witnesses," we seek and accept the prayers, the counsel, and lifestyle of the kingdom. And each lives and works as a partnership within their supporting family.

Commitment to creating authentic power is a marital benefit. Two partners come together. Spiritual partners commit to aligning their personalities with their souls. The benefits of being in a happy marriage are as many as particles of sand on a beach. Marriage provides countless opportunities to expand in love. Oneness expands love for yourselves. Every job is in a constant state of change. We experience more trials and errors than success. In our oneness, even our human mistakes color our decisions, and add or subtract joy from our work.

Love is not a feeling. The love in oneness creates an elimination of constraints. Meaning is revealed as you travel together in one direction. That life journey makes life worth living. God has declared that each of you are worthy of living it. The healthiest parts of your personality are honored. In oneness, we are made whole.

Stephen Covey says every family needs a mission statement. That statement's goal is to enjoy work in gratification. My stated vision for my churches was to create an atmosphere where joy and miracles happened. The concept of service is crucial in our vision and mission statements. These are nothing less than providing for the survival of God's church and every kind of workplace. Couples and groups together should decide on what the faith statements mean.

With the mind of Christ, we focus on objects that are greater than our own happiness. Redeemed people desire to work toward something greater than themselves. They become workers that are like Saint Francis of Assisi, who said, "Go and teach, preach, the gospel every day, and if necessary, use words." Francis lived in sync with his beliefs, his actions, and yes, even his words.

Working together gives a deeper commitment to spiritual growth. When we reach joyful destinations that fill us in ways we cannot imagine. The benefits of working in partnership are undeniable. Nothing is more important.

Life is a love-born passion. We trust that God is compassionate and wise. We ere born for this. Partnerships are arenas for challenging fears and doubts and cultivating our love for others. Building constructive consequences or destructive ones, we are in it all together. Couples must act with integrity, be fair, have fun, and be responsible to each other and to God.

We are embarking in an unknown task. We have never journeyed to the work before now. We need help. We need other people. You and I invest together. We work even beyond the scope of the working tasks given to us by our supervising manager who is God. Integration of love and work involves a tradeoff. In our times, people want to earn a high salary and to work long hours. How does a couple integrate all the work needed in and out of the relationship? Teresa of Avila, who lived from 1515 until 1582, founded the Carmelites.

Among her writings is the *Interior Castle*. The process of loving God to walking through rooms or mansions of a castle. She conceived of seven stages in a soul's progress through death to God.

Going into the castle is the decision to love God. Praying to God is the next stage. Living a life of good works is next. Prayers of recollection and prayers of quiet bring joy. The union with God

Is the betrothal. In the next life in heaven, we have intimacy with God. That perfect permanent union is the spiritual marriage. Teresa called this "an arrow shot by the will." She noted that God's will cannot be coerced by human action. Teresa describes complex mystical experiences that are difficult to understand.

Saint Clare of Assisi (1194-1253) is another mystic that I have profited from reading. Her words are extraordinary and beyond the pale. Clare was the Assisi town beauty. Her father planed for her to marry a man of high ranking. She could have her pick of all men. She rejected all who sought her hand. Like Francis, she left her wealthy home and followed Francis.

Clare's vision was to give back to God the glory of creating us. On her deathbed August 11, 1253, she quietly spoke," Go securely and in peace, my beloved soul. And you, Lord, are blessed because you created me." Few people have ever reached that place in our life journeys. Clare brought new thoughts about the singular glory God imported to God's vision by creating us. (Wendy Murray, "The Radical Vision of Sant Clare of Assisi," The Christian Century, July 28, 2021, pp. 22-25)

Laurel and I have put more than three decades into our marriage. We have tried to work at it as a team. Teamwork is a combined action by a married couple that is effective and efficient. Growing in oneness creates two supporters. Support each other in prayer. Give each other encouragement. Have a positive attitude.

There is a time and place for caution. Curb the automatic responses of discouragement and negativity. Never pretend to be in favor of something you really do not want. Work with a listening ear.

Come to the realization that life is not about our personal ambitions. Surrender those dreams to God. Start building common goals with each other. Working in unity is rewarding to both. We both have personal goals. The strongest marriage team will conclude, "It's not about me. It's about us."

Nurture common interests. Laurel and I were ministry minded before we married. We both grew up in church. Our and our children's lives were directed to spiritual actions. I love working together with Laurel. Doing work in the kingdom of God connects us in oneness.

Where your treasure is, there will be your heart and soul. Your marriage will take root. Stability. Security. Wholesomeness. Longevity. Health. Common ground. Healthy goals. These words define oneness. Read Mark 10:7-9.

Spouses get so entangled in their personal dreams that they will drift apart from each other emotionally. The plan of God for marriage has a strong sense of unity.

I have given you guidance for cultivating a sense of teamwork with your mate. These suggestions for young adults who have not decided to marry will ignite making goals for the future. The whole process of deciding to become a "You and I, Inc." is just plain fun for wise decision makers.

Laurel and I have called each other soulmates. Romance plays an important part in marriage. Passionate romantic love will not promise a long-term oneness. We were teammates from the beginning. We hit the nail on the head. That is why we are where we are.

Picking your partner for life is the most important choice you will ever make. We work as "you and I, inc." because we are teammates. Laurel has suggested that marriage is hard work. Couples must stand together through many difficulties. Challenges are a normal part of any relationship.

A challenge is something to overcome. We have to nourish it.

It is so easy for a couple to become out of sync. They must be tighter allies. Allies communicate and defend each other. They coordinate all their efforts. It is like a three-legged race. Pushing ahead and refusing the partner's cooperation makes both fall down. Work together and both do well. Character speaks far louder than any sermon or book. Character is far more important than her skills or formal education. Character traits that I have attempted to share such as humility, courage, integrity, and passion for others. Character is essential to being a visionary and being a part of a team. Character makes decisions fun. Deciding from inward character mirrors the joy found in playing team sports.

Last year I watched the Kentucky Wildcats basketball team. Every one of their games were televised. Traditionally, Kentucky adds excitement to college basketball every year. Ranked number one at the beginning of the season, they ended up not ranked at all. In the heat of stiff competition, they lost game after game even with great talented recruits.

In an overheated game with Alabama, two tall players reached for a rebound. They battled each other for the rebound. The coach yelled, "Guys, you are on the same team." The player heard the coach. He realized what the two were doing and let go of the ball.

Spouses forget that they play on the same team. Their fates are linked. Laurel and I cover each other's weaknesses. We reinforce the strengths. The joys of being together is a bonus.

Trust is the foundation of marriage. We are committed to honesty that we will not break the faithfulness in our lifelong love. Communication involves feelings, joys, ideas, opinions, and plans on a regular basis.

Communication establishes the connection that allows us to understand each other. Conflict and tension cause couples to work against each other. Coordination is the key to completing plans, finishing projects, and creating oneness that knits our hearts together.

Consideration of each other is vital. Consideration. Feelings. Needs. Desires. Wishes. Respect. Preferences. Laurel has given back more than I have ever given to her.

She has made a positive impact through her love. We pray our incorporated lives have touched the world for good in committed faith hat will ripple on long after we are gone.

Couples need vision and clarity. Without these there is no goal, no direction. Dreams give us clarity. With excitement and anticipation, there comes determination and satisfaction. We need the passion and courage to make dreams together. Getting too busy hides the light of God's love under a bushel. Read Matthew 5:14-16. Jesus is telling us that the resources, the God-given talents, gifts, and graces have been entrusted in our hands. The words from Psalm 103:15-16 convict us that we will soon be forgotten for not setting spiritual fire to create a lasting impact.

I pray my writing books, teaching and preaching faithful sermons, will be passed down through generations as our children and grandchildren continue our work for God's glory. I pray the Holy Spirit will blow upon the embers of our souls to build fire inside us to shine the light of God into all the lives we have touched and encountered.

Relationships are to be rich, fruiting, and rewarding. Strong. Supportive. Loving. Fun. Work in oneness in our efforts will make the impossible possible. Not only will we impact our own family, but we will also enable our neighbors, friends, work colleagues, and those people placed into our journey to experience the joys. I can already see in our children and grandchildren that they will carry forth the joy of having gifts, integrity, decency, and kindness. We want to strive to be people they can trust. That trust brings respect.

When we were young children, my brother Ed and I walked to the Cameo Theater in Bristol to see the Disney movie, *Snow White and the Seven Dwarfs*. We loved the smiles of the little guys as they went off to work. On our way home we sang "whistle while you work."

Dr. Charles Mayo coined the phrase, "There is no fun like work." This quality hospital system based in Rochester, Minnesota attempts to serve medical needs with unchanging ethical principles. People travel from the nations throughout the world to receive quality medical care. Printed booklets from Mayo Clinic are among my most valuable resources n my ministry as a licensed mental health practitioner.

One of the joys of my work is my encounters with college and seminary students. I have delivered 105 baccalaureate sermons for high school students. One of my favorite endings is to share Rudyard Kipling's poem "If."

"If you can keep your head when all about you
Are losing theirs and blaming it on you.
If you can trust yourself when all men doubt you,
But make allowance for their doubting too;

"If you can wait and not be tired by waiting,
Or, being lied about, don't deal in lies,
Or, being hated, don't give way to hating,
And yet don't look too good, nor talk too wise:

"If you can dream—and not make dreams your master;
If you can think and not make thoughts your aim;
If you can meet with Triumph and Disaster
And treat those imposters just the same;

If you can bear to hear the truth you've spoken
Twisted by knaves to make a trap for fools,
Or watch the things you gave your life to, broken,
And stoop and built them with worn-out tools:

"If you can make one heap of your winnings
And risk it on one turn of pitch-and-toss,
And lose and start again at your beginnings
And never breathe a word about your loss.

"If you can force your heart and sinew
To serve your turn long after they are gone,
And so hold on when there is nothing in you
Except the will which says to them: Hold on.

"If you can talk with crowds and keep your virtue,
Or walk with kings, nor lose the common touch;
If neither foes nor loving friends can hurt you,
If all men count with you, but none too much.

"If you can fill the unforgiving minute
With sixty seconds' worth of distance, run,
Yours is the earth and everything that's in it,
And —which is more—you'll be a man, my son."

(Rudyard Kipling, *Classic Poems*, New York: Random House, 2006)

Being a person, my son/daughter includes the pleasure in taking a risk. Joy springs from creating a piece of excellent work. Walking and talking with crowds brings the joy of feeling that what I am doing each moment is astonishing unique. No one else will ever be me. No other moment of living the dream will ever be the same as this one.

Being made in God's image, we know God is with us every time we undertake in our courage to live. Every human adventure has its limitations. Humans cannot go beyond the creation. The older we become, the more the tally of abandoned projects and hopes increase. Many will never be accomplished.

Old age arrives slowly. The diminishing capacity for work and elderly declining faculties are real. We can not row against the current of life. Every age has its own adventure. Suddenly, the passion for action dies down. This irritates the elderly. They are a being, not a doing. The adventure is different, but not complete renunciation. The adventure now brings reconciliation with God, with life, and with oneself, putting an end to inner strife. Continuing the adventure, life has another rhythm.

Believers look to a resurrected life. Read I Corinthians 13:12. That life is a mystery. Resurrection is a new trip, a leap into a new adventure. It is a personal resurrection. Our adventure with God continues. Resurrected life is a renewed life. Springing up afresh beyond comprehension. We will share in that glory.

Richard Rohr wrote, "Resurrection is not a miracle to be proven. It is a manifestation of the wholeness that we are meant to experience, even in this world." Resurrection is the undoing of death. Read Romans 6:5. Before the joy of resurrection, pain and crucifixion happened first.

The renewal of marriage is like a resurrection. For new life to break through in marriage, there comes a death. Couples stay stuck because they are not willing to die daily to their old ways of relating. Some give up in despair. Believing things will never change leads to the belief that things cannot change.

Some couples want to skip periods of grief or waiting. If we do not die to the old, we cannot experience the new. The pattern seen in Christ and in nature reminds us that before experiencing new life in marriage, there is death.

My book, *Joy in All Seasons: Walking Each Other Home to God*, has everything to do with faith and marriage. Faith is the cornerstone upon the adventure is build upon. Honoring our commitments is easier when we share our faith. Marriage is a covenant. It is not a mere contractual agreement. Laurel and I agree that our covenant means it is unconditional, permanent, based on love and to benefit each other.

Chapter Seven

SPICING UP YOUR MARRIAGE

We married someone who is imperfect just like us. God has guided me to write this book to spice up your marital relationship. Oneness in marriage is a goal. Contrary to what is the traditional thinking, we continue to enjoy life as a separate person. When both have friends, they spend time with them. People continue to do fulfill their calling. My Laurel continues to play music including the piano, the bells, the organ, and other instruments. She faithfully watches the food channels. She perfects her culinary skills. She bonds with her grandchildren. She labors to distribute food at the community food bank. Laurel knows that coasting is for sleds. I realize my partner has a full life.

One thing Laurel and I have done is celebrate a "love day." It's not like a birthday, anniversary, or anything that involves gifting, a surprise, and a love lifter. One day we just surprise each other with a gift. It might be something we have made ourselves. It might be a book, a pen, or something like a pretty rock. It could be a candlelight dinner or watching a surprise movie. When we travel, we buy a new Christmas ornament. Every Christmas we decorate a tree with ornaments from the many places we have been.

Surprises are the fuel for joy. Sticking a love note into your spouse's pocket or jacket pocket sparks a surprise. Be spontaneous. Surprising your spouse with a special, out of the ordinary activity will spark the flames. Surprise your spouse with a surprise massage. Laurel and I have enjoyed taking cooking classes together. Surprise your spouse with a relaxing getaway together. Going to a bed and breakfast for a weekend will do wonders. If your spouse does all the cooking, make a surprise meal. If you do not have culinary skills, surprise your partner with a takeout.

Give a surprise kiss in the morning. Breakfast in bed is a perfect surprise. Surprise your spouse with a picnic near a stream.

If we suggest that a marriage needs spicing up, most will just say, "We are just fine." We live in a culture where we experience pressure to pretend life is easy. Some think they have their marriage under control. The truth is marriage is complicated. Wayward children's issues. Financial trouble. Fear. Low esteem. More complications than what we perceive on the surface. Discovering how to attain wholeness means uncovering the masks.

Successful spicing up only happens when we stop pretending, we have it all together. A full-time outcome will never come with a part-time commitment.

Every marriage needs new spice. Spice means surprising your mate with added heat. I am blessed with an awesome spouse. Send text messages to flirt with one another. Buy something racy. Laurel wows sexy black. Spice up your hair and make-up. Men, wear some collogue. Old Spice is fine, but you may want to buy something your wife has mentioned a turn-on for her.

One winter Sunday, I could find no place to park my car. I finally drove to the back of the church and parked in the snow. When I was leaving, I was stuck. Spinning my tires only mired me deeper.

Getting stuck in our marital relationships happens in a similar way. We get stuck following a routine, doing the same things, expecting something different. A rut slowing eases un-noticed just like my being stuck in the snow. Life becomes meaningless. Motivation disappears. Inspiration has flown the coop. Falling into a rut cannot be done by spinning our wheels. Do something. Acknowledge your rut. Identify the cause. You might be emotionally depleted. You might make a reckless move. After I got myself out of being stuck, I drove my Toyota straight off the concrete curb on the street and my car fell apart. Modern cars are built to lose the bumper and the parts are flimsy.

My prayer is that this book and my own vulnerability will get you out of the ruts and into the joys. Ask yourself some questions. What is making me so unhappy and stressed? Am I doing things because I really want to or because I think I should? Am I sticking with my relationship because I refuse to waste the time and effort for spicing up my current life? What parts of life have brought me joy?

Once you realize that you are in a rut, you are tempted to make large changes. Radically doing things to spice up your life can end with disaster. Attempt manageable changes. If your work is in vain, this makes it easier to move on to something else.

Go beyond just saying, "I love you." That might become a phrase uttered as a reflex. It loses its impact. What could you say? Try, "I am so lucky to have you." Or try, "You still mean the world to me. Sprinkle in a little phrase that is not predictable. Going beyond the usual "I love you," creates the heat and passion of your unique love.

When your relationship flounders slightly, it is time to spice up and get back to each other's arms full of surprising joys. Laurel and I want what you want. We are in this together.

Wonderful, blissful, intoxicating wish-fulfillment sparks new spice. Life moves on quickly. Slow it down. Enjoy a day of pampering each other. Score solid massage and bubble bath time. Get swept up in love again.

If you know what cause your rut, concentrate on what you know. I knew that parking in the snow on a cold winter's day was risky at best. If you are having a difficult time identifying what got you stuck into the rut, search the reason you are not motivated to change. Carve time for some mindless relaxation. Eat regular balanced meals. Take time off if your ruts are burning you out. Exercise your body. Sleep well. These kinds of routines comfort you. Random acts of kindness toward each other speaks volumes about how much you care.

Unwind. Permit your mind to wander. Sit quietly in a place in nature. Take a nap. Doodle on a blank piece of paper. Zone out the external stimuli. Take the reigns in your rut. You can do more than you think you can. Don't quit.

Laurel's spice jars. Bring more spice into your time together. We have used two spice jars with "hers" and "his" marked on each. We place them on the kitchen table. We fill our jars with scraps of paper to place our wishes. Using the imagination, we come up with helpful thoughts. On the paper we might wish for a breakfast in bed, for a massage, for anything one desires. This brings a little excitement. If a note is uncomfortable, reach in and grab another note. Spicing up your marriage stretches your security zones. Spice jars introduce new imaginative opportunities.

Walking together in wholeness is not a quick sprint or a 110-meter dash. It is a marathon. It's the only way. Stay in the race. Keep running. Spicing up sparks the best version of the true self

Laurel remains independent. She does not walk around holding it all together. Shared vulnerability and humble humanness come with interconnection. The relationship deepens as each volunteer to live jointly and separately. Being more independent embodies freedom. Be aware when enmeshment becomes an unhealthy codependency. Independence can build barriers. Strong, deep, and joyful relationships live interdependent.

Well-meaning couples have fuzzy, mixed-up ideas concerning married love. It is normal to expect romance and all the lovey dovely stuff. That is one big reason we decide to marry. Our marriages are not fading with less passion or romance. Selfish thinking and discouragement when times get hard. Perfect marriages fall on the outside collide on the inside. Love comes first. Spice up your marriage. Pray for each other. Encourage each other.

Spice means becoming aware of your conflict styles. One person cannot change another. Instead of blaming your spouse for your irritability and disappointments in your marital relationship, express how you feel. Spice up by honesty identify your needs. No marriage contains perfect partners. Both are imperfect in multitudes of ways. Spending time with anyone will get on your nerves. God can use it for good. Areas of weakness are identified. We gain humility. Your goal is not to avoid conflict situations. Don't punish yourself when they occur. Process the damage done. Make repairs. Bridge the gap. Casually saying sorry is not enough. Work with your spouse.
Sincere effort to make repairs maintains a positive balance in the relationship. When we sense tempers rising, take a break. Interject humor. Stop negativity in its tracks.

Stretch your comfort zone. The issue is not whether you still love each other. The issue is how you spice up each other with old spice or with new spice. Choosing to love your spouse despite shortcomings will transform your marriage. New spice affects your family for generations to come. Learn to laugh and have fun. Pillow fights, tickle wars, or funny jokes will get you giggling again.

Openly flirt with your spouse. This will let him or her know you find each other attractive. Flirting is an art. Remember when you first met. That technique still works. Smile across the room with a little glint in your eye.

Spice up your time in bed. We have already written about that. Never put a hold on intimacy. If you have been married for a long time, spicing up your sex life will do miracles. Spice up your relationship by being novel and experimental. Add excitement. Be creative. Vary your locations where you have sex. Show affection. Hugs and kisses, linking arms and legs reassures your love for each other. Keep your bedroom clean. Make the bed. Throw out the junk.

Shower your spouse with compliments. Tell her when she looks glowing and lovely. Express gratitude for the little things like putting out the garbage or ironing clothes. Laugh in tough times. I have not turned off my smile as I keep my eyes on Laurel's charms. Humor is a special bond.

Spice up the marriage by buying little gifts like flowers or chocolate. When I am away from home, I buy something for Laurel. As the years pass by, we become comfortable. We might tend to put less effort in our appearance. A committed partner loves you no matter what. Dressing attractively reignites the physical attraction you had when you first met. Hold hands. Display public affection. Your partner explodes with excitement.

At the end of each summer, Laurel and I take notice to change air filters in our furnace. We have the appliances and heating system checked. We realize the wisdom of preventive maintenance. An ounce of prevention is worth a pound of cure.

Marriages need preventive maintenance. Discuss stressful issues before they erupt. Talk about the holidays. Discus the expectations of your family. Fall in love again. Share the costs of celebrating holidays. Read Mark 6:31.
Keep up your courtship all through the years of married life. Spice up the love for each other. Start new habits now. Create a seamless transition into a renewed relationship. Nurture your
oneness. Each person and each couple define what spicing up means. Defining moments are ripe moments. Spice teems with insight. Defining means for nurture eliminates confusion. It untangles expectations.

Spicing up your marriage offers the opportunity to perceive fresh nuances and desires and renewed old sensations, the old spice. We recognize what we are already doing to nourish each other. Imagine then what new spice can create. Realize you are in a rut. Everything looks gray.

Food tastes the same. Each day you feel bouts of boredom. Listlessness replaces life. Routines are prisoning us. Living is not wrinkle-free. That is a rut.

Spice things up. Shake out of the rut. Do something different. Something out of the blue is unlikely. Attempt something new. Sleep on your partner's side of the bed. Throw caution to the wind. Pick a brand-new shared goal. Brainstorm. Ruts come with our dissatisfaction with life itself. Rolling around in the ruts show relationships are not created by themselves.

Your circle of friends, the community you live in, the region you inhabit, and the conditions of the world stimulate the ruts. Bore. Stuck. Lonely. Trapped. Be equally excited as you consider how you got into your situation.

Couples ignore what they have been successful bring joy to each other. In your journal, write the things that your partner does to nurture. Express appreciation for each act. Our unique spicing means working every day to listen, to support, to show love. Taking time for just us brings us into a new bond. (Ayala Pines, *Keeping the Spark Alive*, pp. 124-144) Does the concept of nurturing mystify you? People fear change. A clear request comes from being separate persons. People revert to the status quo.

Start small. Small is beautiful. Melt into a deeper connection. Share anxiety. Give space. Glide into the glow. Love the giggles. Wrap legs together. Do not push. Do not cajole. Imagine your partner in a golden light. Keep it simple.

Keeping a couple's journal could bring resistance. Pleasure and delight. Sensuality. Enjoyment.

Happy days. Accomplishment. Create a record of bliss and joy. Communicate what is happening.

Do this frequently. (John Powell, *The Secret of Staying in Love*, pp. 23-30)

Pick the right time and place. Relax together. Watch your language. Do not interrupt. End with a bear hug or kiss. Keep enjoying soul stroking talks.

Spicing up is the perfect time to share each other's needs. These could include feeling love. Being trusted. Having fun. Being sexual. Being heard. Being authentic. Being real. Being touched. Being accepted for ourselves. Being nurtured. Entire, unreserved, unconditional love emerges from the commitment. The full magnitude is shared in the Song of Songs. "Love is as strong as death. Songs 8:6. The Holy Spirit draws us into the grace-filled, eternal newness of unsurpassable love.

Spicing up your life examines places in your relationship where you feel stuck. See the places that are boring. Share one routine you would like to be more meaningful. Be gentle. Nurturing spice is delightful, connecting, accepting imperfection. Perceive your life together as rhythm. Each couple has their own beat to dance to. Deal with the rhythming conflicts. Life decision rhythms are difficult. Accepting differences brings satisfaction and peace. Be aware of your intimacy dance. Honor your asymmetry. Celebrate differences. Fantasize about the future. Create a dream box.

Spicing up includes renewing of the wedding vows. This ritual could ignite something beautiful.
Getting out of a rut requires visualization of how your relationship and your life can be filled with more joy. Reliving your first date adds spice by remembering how you came to love in the first place. Plan something similar. Make that magic happen again. Laurel and I are constantly looking for more spice. A special note in a lunch box will help. A single red rose is a delight that Laurel surprises me with at the home airport following a flight.

Joy and happiness are essential for a healthy marriage. Happiness depends on what is happening. Joy is an internal emotion. All marriages have highs and lows. Spicing up a marriage brings happiness and joy each day. Joy is on the inside, but it is express outwardly. Joy is something you cannot help sharing. Happiness is acceptance that the negative and positive are balanced. Happiness is a result of situations or events occurring around you. Outside stimuli sparks happiness.

Joy is not only an internal quality, but also an external feeling. Joy belongs to you as fruit of the spirit. Joy can't be taken away. Happiness relies on outside sources. With the blowing of the wind, happiness changes. Still our days need healthy amounts of happiness and joy to keep smiles on our faces.

Chapter Eight

FINDING GOLD IN THE GOLDEN ANIVERSARY

Marriage is being on a team, no matter how long you have lived together. Golden anniversaries are special. The know what joys of marital love look like. Happy couples know they are a team together, no matter what each faces individually.

I bring a personal agenda in writing this book. Convinced that old age should be a time of renaissance, new beginnings, awakened possibilities, I want to give joy to the world with older members of congregations to face the realities of aging. Developing intergenerational ministries will revolutionize the church. Assisting God's older ones with growing old, not simply aging. Faithful aging happens in each moment. Losses overlap. Loss of possessions. Physical losses. Bodily losses. Spiritual losses. Relationship losses. Role losses. All these are realities that occur in the last quarter of life.

The words of ascription from the Killinger novel hits the nail on the hand. "God, who wast old when the world was young and art still young now that it is old." (John Killinger, *The Zacchaeus Solution*, p. 7)

A woman who has been married for 50 years shared, "Love has created resilience in our marriage. That is one of the most important reasons that we both are living happily ever after, enjoying our gold years."

The earthly journey brings surprises. Not all are good. Always kiss each other goodnight. We never know what tomorrow will bring. Unhappiness results as couples of any age ask, "What if there is someone better out there for me?" Some others ask, "Is this the right path for me?"

The answers to these two questions are: "There isn't, and it is."

Older couples declare that giving space is a good thing. Just because we need to spend time away from your spouse does not mean you cherish and love them any less. Perhaps Laurel and I credit still being joyfully married is that we live in a big house.

Savers and spenders can exist. Seeing eye-to-eye on the longer-term financial goals keeps marriage a steady footing. The biggest problem I find in counseling older couples is finance.

Stay on the same page. Don't let money get in the way.

Self-care is pure gold. Restoration acts with your spouse makes the relationship stronger. We have a soothing tub for relaxing. There is gold in being good to yourself and to each other.

What do other couples do to make their marriages last for decades? They keep the romance alive.

They overcome the challenges that most couples face. Feeling desirable and desired needs conversation about what each would miss if the other was gone. Think about your spouse and let them know you are putting them first.

The golden years include the blissful time of the empty nest. There is possibility for a second honeymoon. Couples welcome their new freedom. Adjustments need to be made. Issues such as declining health, grief over peers dying, increased time together, decreased income and much less energy. There are significant times of togetherness demanding tolerance and flexibility.

Finding gold in later life could include new hobbies and interests, volunteering in their church, community, and in other good causes such as food banks. Together they need to deepen their spirituality to help them deal with the losses and limitations of life. There's pure gold in the golden years with less passion but more endurance. Living through valleys of suffering, golden agers exist on a bigger stage. Some say that Laurel and I look, react, and talk like each other.

We conclude that a marriage of 50 years is a marvelous achievement. The gold is in the joy.

Our elders keep repeating the life-long marital secret as effective communication. Their gold is treating the marriage as unbreakable. It is a lifelong commitment. It is not a partnership that ends when the passion is gone. Couples struggle through dry and unhappy periods. Resolving these difficulties gives them the gold of enjoying an intact relationship in later life.

We write and talk about old age in the same way the world does. Older people are not moving toward death. We are traveling toward greater life. We are dead in Christ now and we are alive in Christ now. Life in its fullness is life within us. We might be reaching for another year or a decade. We can rejoice in each passing year. Those who live in joyful hope will dedicate the remaining years to the One who calls us by name. We find rest in the security of knowing to whom we belong, where we came from and where we are going. We belong to an eternal God who is above all and beyond all.

As I reach toward age eighty, four decades, younger people will tease me, "You are not getting older, you are getting better." They are just joking, but for those who live in Christ they enjoy their death. To anticipate death puts life into perspective.

As INFJ and INFP personality types, Laurel and I are quite similar. Marriage is difficult at times for every couple. It is easier with someone who shares your interests and your values regarding issues such as relationship with children after they have lived 50 or more years. We delight in their accomplishments and maturity. Similar couples manage finances best.

Stable older people urge marrieds to apply what they may have learned in their work, sports, and the military to the dynamics of married life. Setbacks, sudden illness, and difficulties experienced by one team member is the other's responsibility. In family therapy with older adults, I have discovered quite a few married at young ages. They declare the opposite is better.
Seniors advise waiting to marry until each gets to know the other. Shared experiences expose those who think they can change each other.

Learn each other's love language. What a privilege to touch with our hands, our lips, and our bodies upon another's body. Deepest joy demands deepest presence. Love means reverence to the one with whom we have journeyed into divine union with. That union is the pathway to the infinite to love, to God. Connecting to divine love requires a slowing down. Find the gold within ourselves. Find the potential to create. Know the essence The gold of God is never found in our accomplishments, our rewards. Even if your partner continues to say, "I love you," we might not know the joys of the divine unconditional love. We are never too young to challenge old ways.

Our infinite God appears during our slowest moments. God is in the stillness. Explosive joy comes in absolute stillness.

Older couples experience love, freedom, and openness. Imagine what is possible. Think about what drew you to each other in the beginning. Pondering those memories sets off the power.

Days of struggle. Days of contentment. Stop. Breathe. Reflect. Be grateful. Infuse hope. Rewind the life video to view your initial attraction. Fascination. Shared faith. Common interests. Purpose. Comfort. Attraction. Adventure. Fun. Share the reflections in your golden age.

Joy has ebbed and flowed. Despite this reality, older couples keep intimacy vibrant as they age. I have never heard a stock answer. The effects of aging need not create disconnection. Becoming an older couple and the less they can do from a physical standpoint, does not mean you cannot nurture closeness and oneness. Remember your first years of marriage. Both were sexual athletes. Trust me. We will never reach that explosive frequency again.

Older people can have genital sex. They can delight in orgasm. Without a sex life you are warned that you risk all kinds of illnesses and ultimately senility. Any teaching including conservative church dogma about how we should feel about our bodies degrades sex. Active sex keeps your eyes bright, your skin smooth, tissues supple, and hair glistening. Sympathetic magic.
Toning up for passionate action. Women and men make camouflage the aging process. They act out a flaming pantomime which mimics themselves when they were still young. Women regularly visit their hairdresser.

Statistics and university research clearly show that extramarital sex increases in older people. This indicates that older people become freer sexually. From my experience in psychotherapy, I think the rise reflects the greater losses of the elderly and a need for intimate bonding. This is also part of the eternal longing for a lost Eden.

Perhaps couples need to ask, "How are we doing in sexually?" Extramarital sexual affairs at any age will never enrich a personal relationship while married. We are "one flesh" until we die.

Judith Viorst wrote, "It is our attitude to our losses as much as the nature of our losses which will determine the quality of our old age." Loss is part of our life from birth to death. Life still has meaning. For millions of people golden years bring unemployment, inadequate economic support, social isolation, material deprivation, poverty, and starvation. (Carrol Saussy, *The Art of Growing Old: A Guide to Faithful Aging.* 40-43)

Losing one's physical appearance sucks. Sensory. Heart. Lungs. Skin and tissue. Musculoskeletal. Nervous system. Reproductive system. Genitourinary problems. Loss of energy is a loss of self-esteem. Loss of memory is disorienting. Bundles of money are spent by older adults to slow the signs of the golden ages.

Old faces turn multitudes away. Ultimate beauty inside the soul is not realized. Loss of health. Health loss becomes increasingly a huge threat. I recall when I suffered pneumonia and blood clouts in my lungs. Painfully I reflect on that time.

Recall a time when you felt miserably sick. Food was out of the question. Sleep was fitful. Days may have dragged by. Each day you felt little improvement. You wondered how people around you could manage to get up and get going. You wondered if you would ever know energy and good health again. How would you describe such illness? Endless hurting. Weakness. Hopeless. Purposeless. Wasted. Feeling unloved. Despaired.

I have driven more than a couple million miles during my preaching and teaching ministry. Loss of the license and ability to drive would be devastating. Driving was a milestone that I celebrated. My daughter Linda smiled in joy when I gave her my Mazda. Giving up your car keys is a dreaded milestone.

Relational losses from deaths accelerate. Elders over eighty recite litanies of those who have gone before them. There is now a short list of surviving family and friends. I had the unique privilege to move back to my hometown in 1996. I was so proud and honored to be appointed as pastor of Saint Luke United Methodist Church in Bristol, Virginia. My uncles and aunts, my parents, my school mates from kindergarten through Tennessee High School lived there.

My dreams for the church never materialized. Laurel was anxious to move to her family in Nebraska. God moved as the sickness and death of Laurel's mother and no support of the district superintendent was gold among the wrenching disappointments. None of my family lives in Bristol now. All died. I conducted 12 of their funerals. Each was difficult.

Retirement from ministry or any other vocation means loss of your main role. The countdown has come. My days are numbered. I continue to preach as supply. In Nursing homes. In jails and prison. In weekend conferences and retreats. On campuses. For baccalaureates. For weddings and funerals. Old soldiers never die. Neither do preachers.

I write books such as this one. Retirement brings identity confusion. I feel isolated. I feel dispensable. I am alone in my quest for a joyful life.

Research shows that retirees lose an arena for making friends. I still am active in a Clergy Support Group and a group for those who have retired. Ministry became for me a base for self-worth. It was a source of recognition. New experiences, creativity and the use of my gifts and graces were a part. I was given an opportunity to serve others. Nothing beats giving the time of your life to what means so much, you will work for no economic support to experience the joys.

With my retirement friends I brainstorm a list of the major losses. Looking over that list, share the loss you are now struggling. What roles will you never let go? Note any gains you have experienced. Grieve the losses that were left unfulfilled. Joyfully celebrate the gains. What have we enjoyed as we gave up being able to be together? Some people live alone. Others feel lonely.

In my retired preacher's support group, some feel like what the Beatles sang in "Eleanor Rigby."

"Father McKenzie, writing the words for a sermon that no one will hear. No one comes near." I have written thousands of sermons that many have gathered to hear. Ministers know the answer to the chorus. "All the lonely people, where do they all come from?"

Being alone is not wrong. Being alone is part of spiritual life. Spiritual giants, across religious traditions spent significant time alone. Moses. Jesus. Desert monks. Buddha. Being alone brings spiritual life. Being lonely yields spiritual death. God said in the beginning, "It is not good for human beings to be alone." Companionship and friendship do not alleviate the experience of loneliness. The fate of those who are connected to others is different from those who are lonely. Unmarried people live fewer years. After the death of a spouse, the others is more likely to get sick and die. How many times have we seen that death of a spouse is just days close to the loved one's death? Those death certificates should read: "Died from loneliness."

Life is larger than us. The narrative. The story. The saga. Started before we arrived on earth, will exist long after death. Now that we can re-enter our churches, we are not just re-entering buildings. We are re-entering our continuous history. Now after the pandemic, we can welcome old friends again.

Be aware that you are never alone. Nothing from your past is really gone. Read Psalm 8. Elders are treasures. They are more valuable to the world than all the gold in Fort Knox. The gifts in the golden years include the fruit of the Spirit. Read Ephesians 5:22. These spiritual gifts flourish in old age.

My long-time friend and mentor recently reached the age of 88. He is particularly inspiring to me and to Laurel. He keeps up with his many students. He is an active retiree seeking opportunities to give himself in service. He rejoices with those who rejoice. He weeps with those who weep.

Dr. Killinger continues to dream dreams for tomorrow's world. He continues to be responsible for the common good. His has a seasoned sense of what's worth knowing and doing. He has hung on when life was grim. Read Psalm 100:5.

Human beings are always in process. Change is a given. They are shaped by the relationships that reveal who they are. We relate to ourselves. We relate with others. We relate to our spouse. We relate with nature. We relate to God. Sharing the whole life story with others is the essential part of our becoming. One of the enjoyable things about watching "Roots" on television is to realize that everyone has a story. Everyone is a story.

People who live in nursing homes, prisons, or state mental institutions enjoy telling their story. I patiently listen to some of their memories a dozen times. "Just sit down and talk with me" is their continuous refrain. I have their stories from residents from 44 to 104 years of age. I view them sitting outside their doors visiting each other. They greet everyone who passes by. They want to share their rooms. They share family pictures and a few things that have been part of their life story. Read Psalm 16: 9-11.

Reflect on what you enjoy most in life today. Let thanks fill your soul. With joy and wonder, invite words or images to bubble up into your consciousness. Repeat Psalm 16: 9,11. Laurel likes to put her joy to music. Enjoy the surprise and delight that lives in you. The Spirit brings satisfaction, availability, and appeal to every person.

Old age is a fruitful time for spiritual development. Faith works. Faith enables us to recognize blessings in their own lives. Faithful folks suffer less depression. Faiths brings social support. Faith enhances life. Faith brings comfort and joy when we are most in need. Faith shifts from doing to being as we approach frail old age. Faith increases joy with integrity in simple pleasures. Faith accepts life as it unfolds. Faith opens us to the mercy of God.

Be faithful to the faith. The concept of retirement is not made clear in scripture. We can never just coast along. Coasting is for sleds. Scripture magnifies the value of older people. So much wisdom is housed inside of them. Paul summed up his approach to the last days of his ministry. Read II Timothy 4:4-8.

Coasting along causes us to look to sedate and selfish living. Paul said he was "faithful to the fight." Fight is the term Paul sed for his ministry. The world needs the wisdom of seasoned leaders who have served on the battlefields. Paul remained faithful to the finish. Read Philippians 3:14. Image a runner completing a marathon. The committed ones are still exerting the full effort with all the strength they have left. We must finish what God has started.

Stay fresh in your personal and spiritual growth. Be fresh and open in your quiet time. Never use age as a cop-out. God calls us to stay faithful not just when we get tired or retired, but until we expire.

I shared a poem by an ancient poet named Kalidasa who composed poignantly related thoughts in the fourth century in India.

"Look to this day,
For it is life, the very breath of life.
In its brief course lie
All the realities of your existence.
The bliss of growth,
The glory of action,
The splendor of beauty.

For yesterday is only a dream,
And tomorrow is but a vision.
But today, well lived,
Makes every yesterday a dream of happiness,
And every tomorrow
A vision of hope.
Look well, therefore, to this day."

Finish the course. My grandson Ethan and my daughter Linda completed hikes around Montreat Conference Center in North Carolina. On the top of a high mountain, they could see Montreat and the Ridgecrest Baptist Conference Center simultaneously. When I spent my summers living at Ridgecrest, I hiked with college student staff climbing a high peak in the Blue Ridge Mountains. All but one of the hardy, healthy youth reached the top. The straggler kept repeating, "I'm exhausted. I just can't make it." She kept reminding herself that the view would be worth it.

Before sundown, she summoned up one last ounce of energy. As she breathed in the magnificent beauty, she said, "The difference was worth the distance."

Faith is tested by the suffering side of aging. Caretakers provide soothing balm. With those who do care. As we face painful realities, we need to lift our souls above the struggle. Don't just coast. Don't get side-tracked. Don't miss the reward and the joy waiting for you at the end of your life race. As old Rupert Smith, our track coach at Tennessee High School in Bristol would instruct, "Run all the way through the tape."

Coasting is for sleds.

How will I live until I die? Read Matthew 26:38. The dying need the assurance of human connection. **Faith is rooted in reality**. Faith results in deeper satisfaction in the present, as we age gracefully. People age as they have lived. Some seek far more social interaction than others. Old people want gradual change. Aging is highly individual. Sudden changes result from illness and disease, not from. Aging itself. Memory declines. Knowledge increases with these wise ones. Changes in exercise and diet, awareness of healthy eating, enables a high quality of life for seniors. Imagine your eightieth birthday party. Who would be there? What will you look lie? Will any other octogenarians be there?

Leap ahead one decade and think about you at ninety. Ask yourself the same questions.

Identity and significance keep hope alive. Faith, for me, is staying in contact with older adults in my service that is more needful to me as a minister than it is for others. Most ordained pastors have lived in a parsonage much of their lives. When I retired, Laurel wanted to build a custom-built dream home. Our new home is the centerpiece of our days. As most women, Laurel valued security, comfort, and beautiful surroundings. Laurel attended to every detail of her dream home. I used up much of my personal savings to pay for our dream home.

Property taxes have escalated in Nebraska. Home insurance is high in price. Maintaining our home requires energy. Ownership of a home requires more than most couples possess.

Life in the present. Our present life is composed of many things. Work and play. Meals. Solitude. Interaction. Service to family. Engagement in community. Rest and exercise. Reading. Studying. Praying. Well-connected people of all ages live with more enrichment and joyful satisfaction than the isolated people who have few if any intimate relationships. Centering the present life on God determines the strength of life.

Remaining young and healthy is unrealistic. We might remain quite healthy, but they cannot be young again. If you remain physically, emotionally, and spiritually healthy, you can experience miracles.

Laurel and I take time to review what life has meant for us. We discuss any changes in our plans. Read Psalm 104:30. We let our imaginations roam as we live through our days, how we can become engaged in our world. Use your imagination to envision the details what you want the coming years to look like. This makes it more likely your future story will happen. Some great things just fall into some people's laps. Most must work hard to achieve what they want to accomplish.

For us living in a committee relationship, the changes that retirement bring will affect both partners. If both members retire, the change in the family system is even more dramatic.

Successful retirement requires a conversion. We turn away from the familiar to embrace a new life with a different future. The word retirement has negative connotations. The elective years. Renaissance. Recommencement. Reengagement. Re-tire. A wise rebirth. Retirement is long on hopes. It is short on details. How can you write an autobiography or a saga on what has not happened yet?

Retirement adds challenge and anticipation to life in the present. List in your journal ten things we desire to do before you die. This list will give you clues about your future. Consider how your future story has changed since you reached into adulthood.

You can age with vision. Hanging on. Living positively. Thriving. Prayerfully. Wide eyed. Moving ahead. Zest. Creatively. Intentionality. People whose parents died before old age wonder if they will experience more years than their parents.

Future stories assume a long and healthy life. Reaching a desirable level of financial and professional success is the theme in our future stories. The true self is embedded into the stories.

These stories can produce fear or treat. If the future story dies, we grieve. Past and present realities must now be integrated with future hopes and dreams. Believers see beyond the despairing void. We believe in an infinite God on the other side of finite life. That belief and faith in personal eternal life lovingly and successfully completes the future story. Faithful aging means reframing retirement as a time for renewal.

Look at your collections of family photographs. I have at least four photo books that were taken from every ministry place I have served. Reflect on what you see. Recall the people and events remembered. You will better understand them in a new light.

You might visit, make a phone call. Write a letter or email. Accept an invitation to preach at a church homecoming. Exchange photographs. These are ways to bring your past into your present. The brevity of life is the motivation to review life. Unresolved issues can be resolved. We grapple with our past to make peace with it. Life reviews are empowered through the discovery, conflict resolution, and integration that retelling the story gives to the storyteller. Every revisit gives new insight. God's light will shine on unfinished business from the past. Unexpressed pain and anger see the light of day.

None of the emotions experienced in the present or past need be rejected or repressed. Our life tapestry includes love and hate, fear and courage, joy and sorrow. Any abuse or rejection experienced in the past is neither accepted nor treasured. Despised. Protested. Grieved. Shared.

Disapproved. Healed. Survived.

Survivors of abuse reframe the abusive relationship. They focus on their survival skills and their strength of character rather than remaining rapped in the abuse.

Imagine your life as a spreading tree. I like the animation from the television show on our genealogical roots.

Also, imagine life as a flowing river. View the life journey as a winding road. Quickly, we return to the past when the events occurred. Recall your life at that time. List and reflect on the people who were important in this period of your life. Note significant steps that led to this event. Were you appointed to give your gifts and graces in that strange place? What were your hopes and dreams?

Resolving any conflict in difficult past encounters, you will discover the power and joy of positive relationships. The past can then be of more use. Our past covers all our lived experience. When the bishop appointed me to serve six congregations in the Blue Ridge Mountains in Virginia, my mentor, Dr. John Killinger told me to "preach the hell out of those six churches." In less than fifty years, you will not be there. And neither will they."

We find what needs to be revisited. What needs to be reactivated. Reframed. Reinterpreted.

Prayerfully and forgivingly deal with the disrespect, the rejection, abuse, or abandonment.

Working out a solution to a problem, couples get stuck in blaming, miscommunication, and not being clear about what is really going on. I have used the following model for problem solving that you may choose to follow. In the beginning of a session, the couple and I outline the problem according to needs. We brainstorm all solutions. This is not when we evaluate the solution. We can evaluate in a later session. After this evaluation, the couple chooses one solution that is acceptable to both. They then decide when and how to implement the solution.

If they indicate their solution is working, re-evaluate it.

Write down every idea. Even if it appears ridiculous or impossible, consider eliminating those solutions that are unacceptable. My therapeutic goal is to find a solution where each spouse feels comfortable. Getting a winner and a loser is ineffective. When both feel like winners, we have done some good work.

This model builds trust. Both can visualize their problems are manageable. Couples communicate what they now believe. They engender hope by being honest, vulnerable selves.
Positive reinforcement lessons complaining. This involves asking the couple to pray and imagine what their marriage adventure now is conceived. We dare

to live the dream when we believe it is a possibility. Building trust is important. When one spouse shares fears, be supportive. Create a safe atmosphere so communication takes place.

Giving feedback is a device which enables a couple to learn how well behavior matches the intended message. Ask the couple to be specific, not general. Talk about what's happening now. The needs of both are considered. If not, one will be hurt. Criticism is not allowed. Use the "I" messages. Discuss issues that can be affected. If the husband's loss of hair bothers his wife, he cannot change that. Help not asked for is no help. Use finesse.

Reconnection is possible. Touching two separate individuals brings trust that it is safe. Reconnection is knowledge about oneself, so that connecting is comfortable and secure.

There is no automatic model. Each walk away feeling like a winner. Both see themselves as humans with similar fears. The trust becomes so complete that if your spouse could read your mind, it would still be safe.

Reconnected marriage is a mystery as to how the couple now has so much going for them. Reconnection does not look like any other marriage. Two people have hammered out, designed, and constructed a miracle together. Joy comes from the new oneness in an atmosphere of fleshing love.

Chapter Nine

JOY COMES IN THE MOURNING

Mourning our earthly beloved comes best while they are still alive. Otherwise, grief does nobody any good but the one left behind, families, and loved friends. Give one kiss every day. With each kiss, a tear waters down the cheek. We grapple with remorse before we celebrate the oneness. Give the flowers and presents now. Later comes too late.

Loss comes to all the eight billion of us now living on this planet. It can be devastating. God can assure us organically. Losses can create compassion. We become wiser on the other side of sorrow. Grief tends to linger. Mourning achieves nothing as grief refuses to be resolved. Grief stays past its due. Stolen vitality. Choking possibility. Lessoning hope. We ache as life seems that we will not see joy again. Read Job 23:10. The Book of Job lets us know that God will test us. How long must a goldsmith keep the gold in the fire? He keeps it there until he can see his face on the gold. God keeps shaping us until our Lord can perceive our redemption.

Unless we deal with loss, we will have a miserable life. Mourning can be a positive renewing of our best selves. It is possible tat we end our habits of complaining. We lose our tendency to judge. We save ourselves needless worry. We lose our feeling of uselessness.

Death may be another birth. If we knew our loved ones were being born, by death, into a realm of endless joy, faith in our eternity, then mourning would result in joy. We dare stand in the light of truth, and we claim the ultimate treasure. Death is a mystery unanswerable. Death is a wound. It heals slowly, over time. Joy comes from the inside out. During our mourning time, joy is a speck in our rearview mirror. Nature shows us that death is unavoidable. Death should nourish life. Nothing exists in a vacuum. Every action has a reaction. Our choices matter.

Our instinct for adventure is closely related to the instinct of death. Death haunts the mind of everyone. Death prompts us to make a personal mark that will be remembered years after we are gone. My wife has believed in my adventure. Some wives stand in the way. Laurel has encouraged me by saying the adventure is now ours. Happiness and joy come into marriages in which both husband and wife live the same adventure together. It is amazing how it strengthens the bonds uniting them.

During my adventure, as long as I was alone, writing in my home office, it was me living a dream. Adventure must be incarnate. Adventure is facing up to the world and its judgments. Adventure includes special bonds forged between those engaged in the same adventure.

I have learned more than I can put in pages. This learning has included both writing and speaking. It is not what I say or write that really counts. What my readers hear and understand is my and my Lord's goal. I am aware of the power of words and that God uses the foolishness of preaching to bring our salvation. Healing mourning gives us a new opportunity to learn. Time to laugh. Time to struggle. Time to lose. Time to fail. Time to get up again. Time to persevere. Time to get to know God in a personal way. We need to open our eyes to the possibilities. We are our own story.

Breathing air and releasing it is a metaphor for loss and gain. Only by letting go of one breath can we breathe again. It is the breath of life. Let go of the negative thoughts and let a positive one take its place.

Broken attachments grieve for lost love. Powerful emotional reactions come with the mourning time. Attachment theory deals with separation and loss and love. If loss of a spouse occurs abruptly, the typical reaction is a separation distress. Tension. Anger. Anxiety. Disturbed sleep. Restlessness. Difficulty concentrating. These reactions seek to regain the lost attachment figure. They appear as rational in situations where contact with the lost figure is temporarily or permanently impossible.

Life is a process of growing older. Death is on the horizon for everyone. As we live, we age. Intimately connected to the human body, nobody avoids it. We mourn our coming death.

Earthly possessions are swept away. I have saved all my published books, my sermons, hundreds of photo books, travel souvenirs, cards, emails, newspaper clippings, magazines, even my Baptist Press stories, gifts from my family and friends, plagues and rewards.

Most will never be remembered. Nothing will go into a personal museum. I am already giving away many things to churches, goodwill centers, and younger people going into ministry or psychotherapy. Dirt and worms will close over our skin and bones. The flame vanishes. The earthly body will be like a dry brown leaf that crumbles and goes away. We cannot take anything with us. As we age, there comes a stark reality that we must simplify our lives.

The most effective way to live our lives is to discover what lights your fire. Fan that flame.

Pay close attention to specific activities that enliven us. Remain curious s a child. Unattended curiosity eventually sputters out. Fan the flames of optimism and positivity. Nourish all your relationships. Fan the flames of your spiritual life. This is the day the Lord has made. Yesterday was not the day. Tomorrow is not the day. Tomorrow will come as a surprise. Nobody has a crystal ball. Preoccupation with tomorrow distracts us from the present. We will never find God by gazing into heaven. We cannot stick our heads into clouds. Pay close attention to the joy in our lives that brings us love, and compassion. Joy always comes as a surprise.

The gift of all the years we live is not just staying alive. It is a gift of grace. It's becoming more fully alive.

Death is a mystery. The most awesome events in my life have been conducting thousands of funerals. Before our eyes we see the extraction of a loved one. Death is a deep miracle and mystery. Nobody argues about the existence of death. Slowly, we become fully aware. The tension of dying mounts in our every cell. Finally, the reality explodes inside us. All ambitions and our deepest desires, hopes for success, aches for love, and living forever become illusions.

When my mother died, my father began acting abnormally. People trying to help him understand keep telling him that his wife had died. His reaction was, "Oh no, she is sitting on her chair inside our house." He had placed her picture on the chair and talked with "his wife" each day.

There strange and weird abnormalities happen whenever the means of coping loss indicate a person has not been fully accepting the reality. My day never recovered fully and spent his final days dealing with his illusions in a confined setting in Knoxville, Tennessee.

Our last parent's death hits us the hardest. Our relationship with our parents goes back farther than any other one. Our lives depended on them when we were small children. They are part of your world. When they die, a big piece of our past is lost. Parents are in your memory and in your genes. Our looks, our health, our personalities were shaped by the genes of our parents and ancestors. When my mother died, I still had dad. When our parents die, we know we are next in line. Before my brother David died, he researched and disseminated our family tree and our long history.

History intrigues us. We never tire of thinking about our past. History attempts to reach back to scratch the surface of human origins. We cannot change the past. We cannot live another past.

Being attentive to our past, we are vague about our future destiny. This present moment is the decisive time that consolidates the past. Now is the time for discovering its lessons into wisdom
to transform the future.

Stepping forth in awe and humility, we hold fast to renew our oneness to Christ. All speculation vanishes. We finally see our entire life in the light and truth of Jesus Christ. Christ is our advocate who pleads our case. Love always abides in freedom. Love does not reverse or turn back the choices we have made regarding Christ and his offer of grace.

Disgust, fear, and bitter resentment. No surprise, tragic ending. Death can come any day. This is the reality of millions. Black empty space. The fire has gone. Death arrives when we are most prepared to love unconditionally like God. Marriage and death become a pair of lovers. Faithful people stay confident and joyful. As was printed on my brother's funeral bulletin, "Love is forever." David was buried in his civil war soldier's uniform. I wish to be buried with my robe and bright cloth yokes around my neck. Words for the tombstone: Minister of Joy to the World.

Love is a conspiracy against death. In the last moments, we have apparitions of departed loved ones. My daughter Linda and my grandson Ethan received my nurture and protection, my prayers. My love for others gets the better of my death. We die once. The family continues to be visited by death. Beloved others hold death at bay. For those who have been married to God, death is converted into a spiritual spring. Water from heaven gives a mysterious awareness of life.

Couples who suffer miscarriages fear trying again to have a child. A job loss for one or both spouses lead to a fear of never working again. Working through our fears restores hope. When my parents and my brother died, I asked myself where God was in my mourning.

Mourning our loved ones while they are still living brings hope and joy. Death loses its sting. Eulogize them now. Give them flowers today. Believers in the resurrection live a healthy and abundant spiritual life. As death comes, we shall be born in a new form. Life is a gift. Life is joy. Life is everywhere.

Fulfillment and happiness. Blessed assurance. Eternal legacy. We are now ready to continue love.

Love with God will be a perfected love. When Jesus said that there would be no marriages in heaven. He believed that we are all God's bride. Love will be experience with all the citizens of the heavenly kingdom.

Humans handle loss through gratitude for what was good. We accept the realities of what is.

Believers reframe negatives to positives. This part of mourning is not suppression or denial. We decide to focus on negative perceptions in the limits of time necessary.

When we lie on our death bed, I doubt we will be thinking about our comfortable home, our dependable automobiles, clothing, accolades, or fancy jewelry. I know I will be thinking about the moments and experiences that gave me meaning and purpose to my life. These moments will show me who I have been. God made possible our journey into human life. We did the impossible thinking it was just us. Some days were frustrating. Other days were fulfilling. Successful mourning is a harbinger of the joy of heaven.

When we tend a garden, we do not spend time observing the manure. We concentrate on the appreciation of what manure brings into life. Mourning brings mysterious questions. Why is life so brief? Why such beauty? Why live if only to die? Ezekiel knew the answers. He spoke about the mystery of the redeeming love of God. He uses the metaphor as the valley of dry bones. The Lord revealed these things for us to consider for a long hard time life stripped of its breath. In the dryness and deadness of bones is the miracle of the gracious love of God. Ezekiel is communicating that what God has done once, God can do once more. "Can these bones live again? Thou knowest."

Dawn Araujo-Hawkins sees a green or natural burial is an act of faith. She tells of Beth Hoeltke's writing about death. "We have become so afraid of death. We cannot have it in our presence. We immediately call a funeral home to remove the body." (Dawn Araujo-Hawkins, "Green Burial as an Act of Faith, T*he Christian Century*, July 14, 2021, pp. 22-25)

Beth Hoeltke wants a more Christ-like alternative to conventional burial practices. Natural burial is caring for the dead with minimal environmental impact. There should be no chemical embalming, but we need a biodegradable coffin. We can wash and dress our loved one's body in the home. We take them to the grave site. We physically lay the body in the ground. We cover the body with dirt. When death is out of the picture of life, we hand over to someone else. We miss the connection in the ability to love the loved ones through death. Hoeltke's natural burial talks are successful with younger pastors. Ultimately, we are held in God in the earth.

When I die, you might just pump me full of chemicals and place my body in a metal vault coffin, but it's still nothing but dry bones in the end. "Can these bones live again? Thou knowest."

All our personal possessions will be swept away. Our flesh will be required of us. Nothing but bones will survive. Our skin will be blown away. Life will be extracted from us. We will find it hard to imagine. It is a concrete reality. Death keeps building like suspense or odds. The mystery is never understood. Death explodes inside us. Tension continues to mount in our cells. Atoms will go back to where they came from.

The universe is no longer on our side. The deepest human drives are lost. To be secure. To fulfill ambitions. To reach lofty goals. To be successful. To live forever. The drama of living is no longer a surprise and tragic ending. We are forced to face it every day. Humans die a little bit every day. We see death as one black empty space. Just at a time when we have become capable of mature love, we must leave. Death hangs over a married couple like a flame that is flickering out. Death makes love an urgent task. We mourn death at the point we come to accept that we will die. We can do nothing about it. We try to live each moment as if it were our last. Experiencing joy in the mourning. God choose to restrict his human life to just one lifetime. God restricted our lives just the same as that of Jesus.

Marriage is one-way humans choose eternity. Loving faithfully, it is a mystery. Marriage vows create sacrament. Marriage vows are never just some polite agreements. Making vows is a radical leap with one human being and all rest of humanity. We know marriage is a union with God. It is not done during the journey to live a brief time on earth. By keeping the wedding promise, an eternal flame holds the power to enkindle the whole world. The work of covenant is a complete loving relationship. God designed the whole of these earthly days with the intention of sharing with us an eternal joy. In our mourning, e discover that God gives us love that is greater than all other loving relationships. God's gift is our marriage model. Preserve it. Cherish it. Believe in it. In the end we become part of serving as the bride of God.

Love is alive. All the dreams of every utopia do not come near it. A loving marriage is so important as it brings unconditional love into the world.

Imagine holding a flower with unimaginable colors. Each petal is a picture of perfection.

Enjoy this heavenly treasure.

Standing near an ocean beach, look at the sunset. It is almost as lovely as the flower. Immerse yourself in the experience. Breathe with a full deep sigh. Release your exquisite flower into the ocean. Watch it drift into the sunset.

Joy explodes. Watching the flower drift away evokes a heavier emotional experience. Sadness.

Joy and sadness dance within us.

Joy lifts us and dissolves boundaries. We see the oneness of all things. Joy is the most spiritual of all emotions. We feel connected to each other. We connect with God.

Grief hovers over us when we lose something that we cannot get back. Grief helps us accept what has happen. Reality is forever changed. This acceptance and the time of adjustment in the process of letting go. These grieving saps our energy. It brings confusion. This heavy experience is heavy. It immobilizes. It crushes. It appears to be the opposite of joy. This letting go connects us with what is greater than ourselves. We sense an otherworldly time beyond normal space time. That's how we enable our beloved, our spouses, to cross over into glory. Like a river, our tears carry them to the other side. What a mystery that the more we are willing to feel grief, the more we feel joy. Joy comes in the mourning that brings a deep connection. The door opens for us to feel the joy.

Death is total gain. The death of a Christian is precious to God. No death is a surprise to God. God knows exactly when our death will occur. It will come exactly on time. Death is our final act. Death is also a prelude, a beginning, the achievement for us to be made perfect as God intended.

Joy waits until the end of life-affirming grieving. Grief is the internal meaning given to a time of loss. Mourning swifts' grief from the inside to the outside. Joy comes in the process of mourning. Joy is a gift needed to give a break from the trials of life. During the time our family grieved my brother David's death there were moments of laughter between the tears. These tears of happiness prepare those still living to let the moment go. Joy is fleeting by nature Nobody feels joy all the time. Theresa of Avila rose out of her body when she felt pressure during her imaginings. In her imaginative mansions, she lifted upward. When reaching out to God, she never went downward.

Grief never goes away when it is not felt. Unfelt grief weighs us downward. The only way out of grief is through it. If we try to carry unfelt grief, the less we feel joy. Despite some who think joy is not a human emotion, but a mysterious thing that is always inside those who have been converted. Joy is not around forever. We remember joy times in the videos of our minds.

Joy has a dissociative effect according to Saint Teresa. During the process of gaining Oneness with God and others, joy pulls us upward. This is not a healthy place to be all the time.

In my studies at Vanderbilt and Yale, joy was called a "peak" experience. Joy feels ecstatic. Joy is a gift of the Spirit. How special is that! After joy is experienced, we come down and fully inhibit our bodies. If humans were always up, they would not be grounded. There would come a disconnect from reality.

Being anointed by Norman Peale as the Minister of Joy to the World, I and we must be careful with religious teachings that promise joy all the time. Those in denominations that continue to seek "peak" experiences in worship and in prayer groups is elusive at best and sick at worst. Any psychiatrist will tell you that al emotions are transitory. They come and go. Nobody feels angry, anxious, afraid, or guilty all the time. Let joy come as surprise. Live a healthy emotional life.

Dancing with God: A Theology of Joy was one of my many books on joy. The dance of emotions keeps our souls clean and clear. If not this clearing out, we have stuck emotional energy. Imbalance and psychological illness get inside when we try to avoid grief and attempt to feel joy all the time. Mourning is full feeling. It enables us to respond to all that life brings.

Dancing with joy rases the bar for emotional intelligence. Please understand the innate wisdom. Joy is the only emotion needed in heaven. Read John 16:20-24. Anguish and joy are extreme experiences. On the earthly journey, they co-exist. Biblical joy embraces an organic quality by coming to us as a person. Christ is true joy. The Greek New Testament uses the term anguish to define afflicted. Trouble. Burdened. Crushed. Squeezed. Stuck. Persecution. Tribulation. Anxious. Read James 1:2.

In anguish we ignite lack of faith. We cannot see faith afloat. Disbelief attempts to drown us. The experience leads us to deep pain. Confusion. Despair. Anger. Spiritual distress. Prayers appear as evaporated and not heard. Betrayal lurks. Confession. Lies are taken from the heart. Dance. Expect a surprise. Take the crown of beauty instead of ashes. Embrace the dance. Receive the promise. Pour the oil of gladness. Let God shine on anguish. In that moment, grief and joy dances together. Only God can replace our grief and turn mourning into joy.

Mourning eases the memories. Create a memory tree or memory basket. Include the lost one's favorite Bible verse. Fresh flower. Music. Snacks. Fresh pies like the loved one made. As in my brother David's time of death, honors and awards, a basketball signed by Pat Summit and all the Tennessee Lady Vols. As he was a Civil War scholar, his body was dressed in a soldier's uniform. Invest in a cause in the name of the loved one. Offer to take his family to his gravesite.

Send monthly cards during the first year of the loss. Give continuous prayers for joy.

Mourning is never black and white. Mourning brings confusing tension. Pain and joy coincide and collide. We deem it impossible to navigate these conflicting emotions. God invites us to embrace all of it. We all know the joy and sadness dance. C. S. Lewis wrote, "Joy is the business of heaven." God is always present in moments of joy. Read Psalm 16:11.

God gives us reason to rejoice. Joy is the fruit of the Spirit. It is rooted in God. Happiness is rooted in our circumstances. Rushing someone through their mourning short-circuits grief and diminishes joy. Grief will deal with you until you deal with it. Faithful people do not grief without hope. When we intentionally deal with grief, we find knowledge and the best ways to mourn future losses.

Choose to match your sadness with joy. When we lose somebody we love, life will remind us of the bittersweet loss forever. There will be dark days. Dark days are normal. Stick with the promises of God. Do not get stuck in the darkness. The way we love like Christ is to live forward in their light. Honor their memory with love. Create new memories We are deeply connected in our sorrows and joys. Duality is a concept all mourners are familiar with. At any moment we can feel deep sorrow and authentic love, hope, and joy.

During the time of mourning for David, we felt the time was a gift from God. There was more joy and more sorrow than I knew was possible. We cried. We laughed. We talked. We reminisced. We planned. We joked. We grieved. We were connected deeply to our sorrow and in our joy. I miss David and I wish he was here beside me. We experienced a family reunion a year before he died. Thank God. I keep envisioning myself standing beside David as I preached for our family at a Two-Seed-in-the-Spirit Predestinarian Baptist Church located in Cade's Cove in the Great Smokey Mountains. David laughed. We all enjoyed worship in that old 200-year-old pioneer church building.

Times of loss can be times for growth. Everyone mourns in unbearable pain. Mourning brings opportunities to show love, comfort, and support of your partner. Dealing with a crisis involves talking about past losses. Record helpful thoughts in your journal. Focus on the fact that there is light at the end of the tunnel. Becoming overwhelmed by your loss is partly due to our projections into the future. Our confusion causes us to linger in the past. Let go of the tensions.

Let go of the expectations.

Visualize the person so loved coming into the arms of God. Suffering and pain flows out of your loved one's body. See God hugging your love feels assuring. Acceptance. Trust. Nurture. Support. Go with that mysterious flow. Let go of the limiting beliefs that appear under our happiness that shut down the flow of energy.

Spend time sensing the atmosphere. Sense where you are holding on to negative feelings. Focus on the tightness and the resistance that will not let go. Feel the freedom that comes from letting go. Become sensitive and soft at your edges. Let go of the feelings. Become lovingly kind to yourself. (Larry A. Bugen, *Love and Renewal: A Couple's Guide to Commitment*, pp. 10-24)

This poem by Mary Oliver has been helpful as I mourn and enable others to mourn in a manner that ignites fires of joy.

"Who made the world?
Who made the swan, and the black bear?
Who made the grasshopper?

This grasshopper, I mean,
The one who has flung herself out
over the grass, the one who is eating
sugar out of my hand, who is moving
her jaws back and forth instead of up
and down—who is gazing around with
 her enormous and complicated eyes.

"Now she lifts her pale forearms and
thoroughly washes her face. Now she
snaps her wings open, and floats away.
I don't know exactly what prayer is.
I do know how to pay attention, how to
fall down into the grass, how to kneel
 down in the grass, how to be idle and
blessed, how to stroll through the fields,
which is what I have been doing all day.

"Tell me, what is it you plan to do with
your one wild and precious life?"

(Mary Oliver, "The Summer Day," *New and Selected Poems*, p. 94)

Carl Jung said, "We cannot live the afternoon of life according to the program of life's morning, for what was great in the morning, will be little in the evening, and what in morning was true will at evening have become a lie."

Regrets and remembrances, failures and successes, triumphs and tragedies are part of the living of any life. Sometimes our worlds are shrinking. Returning to one's house after a death is hard. Those who mourn must sink into solitude to make progress in grieving. God meets us inside our sacred soul spaces.

Mourning couples yearn for that magic closeness of a spouse, two nestled in oneness like spoons. Sleeping single in a single bed gets old. Sleeping in a king-size bed is sleeping without a king or queen.

A wise grieving woman said it best, "Where you are is where you are. Where you are going is up to you." When our loved ones die, we encounter the world differently. We look at faith differently. The hope and prayer for this book is that the words open faith so it can be visualized trough teary eyes. Step closer to the mystery of our supporting God.

We have been promised brighter days. Though we go through the valley of death, we shall fear no evil, for God is with us. We praise and rejoice in our work of mourning despite everything. Our inner filling with joy affirms our love and our commitment to the love of God.

Our mourning turns to joy. Peaks of immense joy are not unique to the Christian or even to non-believers. Discovering and understanding joy is to tap into the power of God. Renew your mind with the mind of Christ.

Rejoice in the Lord always. "All we know for sure is now. All we remember is here. After the pain and inside the pain, death reminds us to do our best, here and now, and love as much as you can. As much as we can. Over and over, no matter how much it hurts, I can hope there's more, and must live as if there isn't." (Shreve Stockton, *Meditations with Cows*, p. 187)

During his mourning, Stockman wrote, "In mourning, in grief, I traveled to an in-between land. I found myself in a realm between worlds, where the veils seemed to drape right across my shoulders and slide like silk across my face. The familiar world seemed hazy and blurred, as if from across an expanse of altitude or drugs. This world, our world, felt untouchable, but the realm of the departed was untouchable, too." *Ibid.*, p. 175.

Chapter Ten

WHEN JOY BOMBS EXPLODE

The joy experienced during the earthly journey cannot compare to what awaits us in heaven. Certain things invite joy into a marriage. Other things drain out joy. Love is the most important factor in our lives. Without it we are incomplete. Love does not reside solely in a person's subjective thoughts, drives, or feelings. Love results from actions with tangible consequences.

Love brings out the best in us. I love to read and share quotations about love. Actor John Barrymore said, "Love is the delightful interval between meeting a beautiful girl and discovering she looks like a haddock." H.L. Menken noted, "Love is the triumph of imagination over intelligence." George Bernard Shaw wrote, "Love is a game exaggerating the difference between one person and everybody else."

Joy comes from aligning priorities with deeply held beliefs and lifestyles. Joy is a deep connection to your spouse. Joy savors all those moments that make marriage so beautiful.

A simple kiss, a surprise love letter on your pillow, the brief phone call, and other surprises fire the flame of marital love.

Joy bombs explode as we traverse time and space to enter the fullness of God's vision and presence. Eternity is not elongated time for it is both now and the future. Eternal life has begun in time and space. Eternity is the now of human existence. Today we decide for or against the Christ. We juxtapose the *eschaton* and the here and now. The Holy Spirit assures us of a future life if we are faithful and loving in the now time. Eternal life is given to us since it belongs to God. Hope for an immortal eternal life reaches out into the future. That future has already started. It is rooted in the present. The salvation of God is radical. It is simply and purely from grace and unconditional love. Hope, belief, and transcendence are rooted in the faith of God who loves and saves us. We are maturing the seeds of eternity in our realm of time. In an instant, we will complete our conversion to the Christ. Our conversion enables us to die to disobedience and sin, to hate and unlove, so that, like the saving Christ, we live in obedience and love to Christ's brothers and to God.

We do not accomplish our salvation, our conversion after death. Read II Corinthians 6:2. God became a son of God so that the divine in its humanness will create a perfect result. If we are Christ's followers, our own route to God is no different.

Joy is discovered during the process of improvement, effective communication, change, and becoming one. Joy is the strength to stay together on times when the first impulse is to run away.

Joy comes through forgiving each other. Joy is being loyal through thick and thin. Joy champions the cause no matter what.

Laurel and I believe joy of the Lord is the most dynamic gift. Joy turns our mourning into dancing, our despair into hope, and our fear into faith. The essential strength comes from spiritual transformation. In our decades of marriage, we know that joy functions like oil in an engine. We rejoice in our commitment. Joy transcends every moment of our lives. Joy is an emotion, but more than a feeling. We embody joy as we respond to each circumstance coming into the circle of our lives. We have studied joy from every angle, academic and spiritual. Joy emanates from God.

Joy has little to do with making money. The house we live in becomes home. Cars, jewelry, clothes, attractiveness, or world praises are not foundations for joy. Joy is not a sentimental emotion. Joy flow like a mighty river that flows from God from God's loving headquarters.

Read Psalm 9:2, 19:8, 51:12. We have enjoyed our relationship with God. "The joy of the Lord is our strength." God's river of joy will never dry up. It will never be diverted. Joy does not swallow our troubles nor our grief. Joy includes feeling pain and being disappointed or feel rejection.

We shall remain in God's joy. We continue to submit ourselves to the plan and truth of God. Joy is ultimately pointed to gratitude. Thanking God is not always found in human response. Our lives will improve and so will our marriages. We express our thanks to God wit a prayer at each meal. Prayer moves us closer to God. Prayer is the way to intimacy and partnership with God. That relationship in prayer results in our conversion to the transcendent will of God.

Closeness to God brings us closer to each other. When too many days pass since the last time we prayed together, we hunger to approach the Lord.

During our 35 years together, joy has lifted us into a kingdom of God perspective. It is God's intension for all of us to experience abundant joy. Rejoice always giving thanks in all circumstances. We have read that assurance. Putting it into practice will give us a clear understanding of love. In some of our life circumstances, we feel we have lost joy. The good news is that we do not have to muster up joy with our own strength. "The joy of the Lord is our strength." God cares deeply about our joy. God will guide you back to joy.

God never makes a mistake. God is all wisdom. God knows the end from the beginning. God knows the "what ifs" of our lives. Calamities that might occur. Difficult situations are turned into good. In theological seminary classes, students hear the God is omniscient. As we grow older, we see tat God has never made a mistake. Perhaps we will have wait until we get to heaven before we understand some of the bad choices we made and how much God's love and intervention was guiding every step.

As we keep a record of what has happened to us, we observe that everything happens for a reason. God never makes a mistake. When we request God's help, ask God to do what needs to be done. If God were in control of our every action, we would never do anything wrong. With our free will, we realize that God knows the "what ifs" and the outcomes.

We become jealous of other people's automobiles, their homes, their children, their jobs, and their attractive spouses. "Be ye holy as I am holy." Read I Corinthians 13:5.

God is not negative. God Word tells us **what we can do**. Responding to the positive commands of God's Word always is the right thing. Nothing in the Bible is not the will of God.

We need much more than pious, self-righteous religion. Do away with cultural expectations. Surrender to the leading of God. Let go of your own plans. Joy comes from the Lord God. When we let go of our own expectations and interpretations of how God's love works in us, we are free to rejoice. Joy bursts out in heaven with the joy of our salvation. Salvation is God's will. Read II Peter 3:9. God does not superimpose that joy on anybody. The Holy Spirit woos us, but we leave the results to God. Thank God for the "what ifs" that would have caused us to fall were it not for God.

What all the reasons of God are, we will not know until we die and go to be with God in heaven.

Our task being willing to do the will of God no matter what. We must prepare for whatever comes.

We might reach that place suddenly. We might just take many years to realize that God does not make mistakes in our life journey. "All my trials Lord, soon be over." God is working for our good. The will of God is perfect. When we recognize this truth before our trials "soon be over," joy, deep down joy bursts open.

Commitment to the will of God is the way to joy. Accept God's will in every area of your life. That includes your marriage, your calling, your job, your children, your loved ones, and your health.

We will feel lighter. We relax in the love and forgiveness of God. Nothing can keep us from the love of God. We believe God's promises to give a vision of hope in any afflictions. In Christ we are new creatures. His mercies are new every morning. God will never leave us.

Turn fear and worry into prayer. Worry crushes joy. Rejoice in the goodness of God as God carries our burdens. We recover what causes the heavenly emotion. Joy reinforces the graces of our ordinary days. In your journal make a list of what causes your joy. We know the joys are there. We are just too blind to see. Journaling reveals things that pour honey into our sweet moments of rejoicing.

Every life experience is part of our story. Each one is to be celebrated. Contemplate your story. My books and communication set the tone for your story of joy. This is my humble window into my way and the way of God. Being converted or as some fundamentalists say, being rededicated is a return to joy. Returning to God is the same as returning to joy. Returning to God and accepting forgiveness means a reconnection with the Source of joy. We do not have to continue our sorrow and pain. Both repentance and resurrection make things right. We return to joy again and again.

We create our own barriers to joy. I preach joy because I have come to realize that people confine joy. Some are so disconnected from joy. They have no idea what joy feels like. In my on-going research, I collect the things that make people smile or laugh or what gives them a sense of joy. When I taught a class on psychology of joy at Missouri Western State University in Saint Joseph, Missouri, I told my students to do anything they wanted to show me that they understood joy. Some oil-painted pictures. Some danced. Others looked up every verse in the Bible that talks about joy. Ambitious learners wrote pages and pages to write their understanding of various aspects of joy. I instructed them to notice where they go. See whom you are with. Observe what you are doing. These are sources of clues to what brings more joy into our ordinary lives. These moments are often small and fleeting. Joys pass quickly. There is no waiting or searching. Joy will find you.

Once we identify what brings joy, think about intentionally building more of those moments into your life. Sometimes, after all my years of reflection and research, I lose touch with joy. Connecting with the sensation of joy reacquaints with joy. Joy is an emotion with a physical feeling. Joy brings an automatic smile. Joy brings lightness to our bodies. Life expands and radiates. Many have the sensation of feeling warm. Blood flow increases in moments of joy.

Tune back into what happens in your body with joy. Happiness measures how good we feel over time. Joy measures how good we feel in a moment. Milestones are the happy times. Buying a house. Being ordained. Getting an award. Being promoted. And yes, getting married. People often postpone joy while pursuing pleasure and happiness. When we reach that milestone, we want something new. Happiness is elusive. Joy causes happiness to be more attainable.

Joy is the means for connection. Joy is emotional resilience. Joy improves health. Focus on joy and happiness will find you. Children feel more joy than adults. We let go of joy as we age. Spend money on art supplies, dance lessons or a new hobby. We must give ourselves permission to experience it. As we focus on what brings us joy, notice what saps joy. Awareness helps us change and to avoid things that rob us of joy.

Joy is an unfettered moment. Joy feels good. Joy prompts changes. Joy is a repeatable emotion. A joyful self is a true self. Joy is not just something we find. It comes in surprise. Joy is a happy place. Joy is suppressed. Joy is your right. Walking with each other is joy spotting.

Joy is not pleasure or thrills. Momentarily pleasure is not joy. A care-free and worry-free life is not one of joy. Joy is not easy or free of hard difficulties. Joy is always there in surprising ways.

Joy is diminished when we choose things that are not part of my faith, my beliefs, or my values.

Joy is a selfless emotion. Joy is not about me at all It stems from selflessness.

Joy is serving others. It is not taking but giving. Joy walks in patience. Little annoyances slide by instead of festering in frustration. Patience is expressed in kindness.

Being surprised by joy comes as we put down our phones. Laurel and I enjoy simple moments of connection. We wink. We smile. We hug. We tap each other lovingly. Love making is sweet. We regularly say, "I love you." Sweet embraces, followed by kisses that mean something. Our sex life really connects.

Ever since I took a course on psychology of joy at Vanderbilt University, I have collected various people's accounts of joy. Leading lives of deep commitment, I view an explosion of joy.

Joy is a transcendence of self. Self-forgetting. Surprise. A north star. Steer toward joy. Life peaks. Life is full. Joy is a dance. Joy is connected effervescence. Self-consciousness is hidden. Joy is present. Joy is fully alive in the moment.

Joy is a sudden bursting of love. See in a parent in the first time that the eyes see a newborn. When my daughter was born in Nashville, a flood of love and joy erupted. New couples glow across a picnic blanket. Older couples feel that they are deeper into each other than they are in themselves. Lovers are enchanted by a mysterious force. Joy is a mystical attunement. Transcendent joy moments may last a few minutes. One moment alters a lifetime. Joy is a taste of something eternal. Joy consists of a desire for that taste again. Love shines down on us. Explosions of joy energize. We act. We sacrifice. We dare. We serve others. Radiating a permanent joy is loving and serious commitment. Joy flows out of the interiority of the spirit. Joy is delightful, grateful, and kindness together. Joy is self-transcending. Rising unexpectedly, joy sweeps over us. Joy never fades.

Bombs explode our gratitude and appreciation with thank you expressions for the blessings of marriage. We simplify our lives. We fill our space with people and things we love. When I do not feel good about myself, I lose energy, passion, and enthusiasm.

One of my uncles was serving in the United States Navy in 1954. He was on an island in the Pacific Ocean. One hundred miles away was another island. A hydrogen bomb was about to blast in the darkness. He watched the bright light from the distant explosion. He heard the soundwaves booming in the clouds over the ocean. His little island was shaken again and again. With the light of a new dawn, he saw the top of the mushroom rising from fourteen miles away. The cloud was 180 miles away.

The H-bomb is awesome, terrible, and destructive. Blasting off just a few of these bombs could easily destroy the entire earth. Read Revelation 1:17.

For the believer, dying is not to be feared. Even if our death comes by the H-bomb, we will rejoice. Read I Corinthians 15:55. Just the mention of death brings a variety of negative emotions. For those who live in the love of Christ, the experience of death is filled with joy and happiness. At age eighty-eight, John Wesley witnessed visions of angels taking him home.

Norman Vincent Peale exploded with enthusiasm. When Laurel and I participated in Peale's Schools of Practical Christianity, we could feel the intense enthusiasm. It was part of the total commitment that every staff member brought into this positive thinking ministry. When we drove back home from Pawling, New York, we were marveling at the experience. We wanted to go back. Even today, I enjoy playing the tapes of those soul-chilling messages.

Enthusiasm finds the opportunities. Spiritual energy makes the most of them. We can pick up the joy from God from other positive people. We are drawn to them. Happiness. Positive thoughts. Fulfillment. Worthiness. Well-being. Calm. Energy. Ease. Love. These are the results of enthusiasm. Peale said to his flock at Marble Collegiate Church, "Cushion the painful effect of hard blows by keeping the enthusiasm going strong, even if doing so requires struggle.

Marital joy lives in the moment. It means being present. It means laughing in situations that do not seem so funny. Bouts of laughter come as we think about the same thing in the same exact
moment.

Choosing to love brings joy. Joy is all of life. Love grows as we see the talents, marvelous gifts, attributes and personalities that make us who we are. Marriage brings peace, purpose, and comfort in ways we do not currently recognize as possible. Slowing down, soaking up every moment that life offers fills us with happy and rewarding memories for the years to come.

Having joy of the Lord as strength does not mean our lives will be perfect. You will be surprised by perfect moments. Faith gives us happier outlook, positivity, and shear cheer. Fulfillment comes from having some other know me so well. Sometimes that is scary. After years of being together, we have become adept at analyzing facial expressions, tone of voice or mood signs. Couples come to know and understand each other so well that they never have to explain themselves.

Our feisty youth minister at the Christian church in Weeping Water introduced modern spiritual songs into worship. With new people being converted and baptized in the faith, the joy of God had exploded into the community. One Sunday as two whole families were baptized, we sang a song called "Joy Explosion." With pictures of people sharing joys, we sang, "There's a joy explosion. God is in the house. There's a joy explosion, lift a shout. Like a river flowing from the throne of grace, joy is in this place. God is in this place. Somebody testify. Lift your voice to the sky. Fill this place with God's praises. Somebody glorify Jesus Christ the Lord on high. Thank him for the joy that's breaking out in this place."

As I completed the baptisms, we sang, "There's a sweet, sweet spirit in this place."

Enjoy the comfort of having a teammate. Until I married Laurel, I did not realize the value of an effective team. As a first-born child, I preferred doing life myself and not in groups. Our marital teamwork is not flawless. Laurel says, "Jim, this is not a competition. I am on your team. You are the love of my life." Both of us are important to the success of our marriage. Embracing the teammate experience releases pressure on both of us. When one spouse is down and out, the other one brings encouragement and motivation.

Marriage is a ride, a journey, a sanctifying experience. When the joy bombs go off, there is nothing they cannot do. Each is committed to make the marriage wonderful. Joy starts with God in the middle and the Word and guidance of God that is practiced every single day.

God is guiding your marriage. It is more than love for each other. Marriage has a higher dignity.

It holds strength and power. It is a holy ordinance of God. Our oneness is a link in a chain of generations. Love is our private possession, but it is more than personal. Love comes from each of us. Marriage comes from above. As high as God is from humankind, so high are the rights, the sanctity, the promises of marriage. Your human love does not sustain the marriage. Marriage sustains our love.

Marriage awakens every human being to a spiritual journey of love. Martina McBride has shared the amazing joys in marriage.

I have been blessed
And I feel like I've found my way.
I thank God for all I've been given
At the end of every day.

I have been blessed
With so much more than I deserve.
To be here with the one
That loves me.
To love him so much it hurts.
I have been blessed.

The only emotion in heaven will be joy. Love is everlasting. Have faith that those who love each other will dwell together after death. Love remains. All who experience death will be safe and secure. Heaven corresponds with deeper loves within. Jesus promises that we will have a home, gardens like Eden, and friends. Nobody will sit and play a harp. Laurel enjoys playing the harp. She might continue it there.

Music adds grace and beauty. Music transforms the mundane into the sublime into the spiritual.

Music picks up our spirits. I enjoy hearing Laurel play her piano. Go through your current music selection. Make notes about what music enhances or changes moods. Soft, slow music calms. Relaxing music balances your environment. Music warms the soul. Music ignites healing energy.

Successful marriages are active. Each works in harmony with the other. An idle life is dull. Lethargy and self-centeredness replace love. Evil brings its own punishment. Selfishness brings on dissatisfaction and gloominess. Marriages break with selfishness. We blame lack of commitment, finances, incompatibility, infidelity, and communication. Share your hopes and dreams with the one you have been given to love. Give intentional quality time. Quality time never happens if it is absent. Our spouse must be the most intimate and deep relationship. Trust takes quality time. Trust builds after days, weeks, and years of being who your true self is. Trust is doing what we said we will do.
Refuse to place anything in front of your eyes, body, or heart that compromises your faithfulness. Admit that we are far from perfect. Mistakes

are made. Forgiveness is needed. Unending patience is required. Energy, money, precious time. Nice house, retirement account, reliable automobile. Commitment does not depend on these things. Donate. Sell. Recycle. Remove. These actions have eternal rewards. Stuff accumulates. Stuff distracts. Success in marriage does not indicate the right mate. It comes through by being the right mate. Read Proverbs 2:10-22.

Show discernment with the opposite sex. Proverbs 2:10-17. Be alert to flattering speech. Show extreme caution in your communication. Tune in with your spouse. Schedule conversation. Go on dates. Schedule travels. Pay attention. Be alert to your vows. Remember your covenant with God. Fear the damage from improper relationships. The cost is total destruction. Loss of years.

Loss of material blessings. Loss of life. Proverbs 5:1-4.

Commitment has more to do with making marriages work than anything. Futures are tied together. Your beloved will not be here forever. Give your all. Keeping the commitment is even more important than the initial commitment.

"Until death do us part." Sounds romantic. Sounds deadly. It is a serious and permanent commitment. Love is a decision. Love alone is not enough. Act on this decision. Do loving things. Take a walk. Show respect. Speak kindly. Rekindle love again and again.

Love is a mystery. Emotional combustion which bursts the moments of loving joy into a flame for some people. Most of us fall in love with someone that we have served in a non-romantic relationship. Two are transformed in surprising ways. Marriage is a source of joy. Every moment does not ooze with joy. Consistent joy involves keeping in love. It is never just willing joy. If joy is not present, get assistance now. Increase joy if it becomes limited or rare. Forgiving and giving forgiveness brings wonders. Difficult conversations can erase any mistake you have made. Trust is built when couples can discuss those difficult issues that eventually made life miserable. When damaging trouble comes, turn to your spouse. Too many seek wisdom from friends. Connecting with co-workers or so-called friends who think they are liberators.

If couples would discipline themselves to consistently turn to one another first and then to others, joy would increase. Joy often increases when we are on vacation or a study break.

Every day we are bombarded with bad news. Infidelity. Layoffs. Pandemics. Political divisions. Wars. Disasters. Fires. Bad news strikes us in unyielding fashion.

Do what Jesus taught us. Nothing kills God-given joy like disobeying God. Life is found in the things he taught us. Wisdom is to intentionally seek to understand the teachings of Jesus. Joy will flow into the relationship. Jesus gives the ultimate path to joy.

Marriage can be a place where joy explodes. Nobody experiences joy every day. Each season of life brings a deep sense of goodness in the life God has given you. Freedom in Christ is to be free and to follow Jesus. To be free in Christ is to be ordained to the same ministry that Jesus defined in Luke 4:18-19. Jesus calls us to move quietly, not struggling, not straining, not trying to become within the world and the church world. In ministry, in evangelism, in all of life, we are given the time and love to reach out. God knows best how to use each day how to redeem the time. Read John 8:36.

We offer thanks to God for our marriage and for each other. As we reflect on our first glance toward each other, the strains, the misunderstandings, we focus on the joys. Marriage is not created by humans. God brought us together. God worked and forgave us for looking in wrong directions. God continues to weave us into oneness. God accepts our failures. God grants the assurance that there is beauty, purpose, and meaning in this mysterious journey bathed in love.

I served as a volunteer minister to students for Southeast Community College for twenty-two years. I would walk the campus at night, men and women, or even visit them in a place in their college apartment. When I went back home, I would tell Laurel that I was with a student and share the joy of what happened. I had the security of my wife knowing me and trusting me. We are to bring wholeness to people. We must never hurt or abuse anyone.

In doing ministry, we are open to somebody's ego satisfaction. Try to be faithful if you are in a situation now. Once when I worked as a community therapist at Cedars Youth Center, I was scheduled to go into a home for a counseling appointment. When I opened the door, I was encountered with a rugged looking man with a gun in his hand. Not everyone understands faithfulness. The real risk that some people are ought to use you. Be trusted to love regardless of what other people do. People are hungry to be loved. Some come to prefer to keep their relationships sterile, even cold.

Teresa writes about the explosion of rapture. She says our hands become as cold as ice. Those hands remain stretched out as if they were made of wood. The body remains standing or kneeling, according to the position it was before the rapture came. This joy is so excessive by comparison with any other experience on earth, it is a fainting almost completely. It is a swoon. It is a delight. In this pleasurable state, a swiftness of movement carries away the higher part of the soul. (Robert Sternberg, editor, *The Psychology of Love*, pp. 244-250)

Teresa wrote her thoughts in Spain five centuries ago. Her work has ramifications for all spiritually sensitive Christians who live in our modern world. Carefully written documents describe ways of building a personal relationship with God. Sister Teresa discovered ways to organize faith around prayer, solitude, meditation, simplicity, and fresh aspects of spirituality.

In her *Interior Castle III*, Teresa wrote, "Sometimes, when I think of myself, I feel like a bird with broken wings." Teresa inspires us to dream possible dreams. She expands my spirit in a mysterious way with quiet and sure courage. Limits are not relevant to her. God mends broken wings.

Teresa wrote out of her personal experiences. Her imagery resonates with our own souls. Teresa insists on prayer as constitutive to her teachings. Fidelity to prayer flows from the faith-conviction that our soul's center is God. Prayer moves us. Prayer is Teresa's highest recommendation expression of a love relationship. (*The Collected Works of Saint Teresa of Avila, Story of a Soul: The Autobiography of Saint Teresa of Lisieux*, and *Saint Teresa: Her Last Conversations* will transform your marriage and your life.)

The work of Saint Teresa was done at a time when many convents in Spain were riddled with corruption. The church was weak. Teresa was a doer, not just a thinker. She wrote. She spoke. She worked quietly. Common people loved her. Sister Teresa made a deep impression on people around her. The word about her work was spread throughout Europe and to Rome. The church sked her to write down her thoughts and her actions. She felt reluctant to do so. Eventually, she produced a prolific body of written material. She was trying to reform the Catholic Church.

Spain's reformation, unlike that of Martin Luther, has been kept a secret by historians. Luther was expelled from the church. Teresa stayed within the church. Teresa challenged the spirit of the theology of the Catholic church. The reformation in Spain was spontaneous and filled with excitement.

Teresa's reformation renewed the practice of personal spirituality, including the disciplines of solitude, prayer, and meditation.

It is not a mourning or heavenly thinking. She wrote, "It is as with a fire which is large and has been prepare for lighting. The soul has been prepared by God, and like fire, blazes up quickly and sends up a flame which soars high." (Ibid., p. 245) Teresa experiences a levitation. She feels fear as she is lifted off the ground. Without dying, it is impossible to be one with God. Suspended between heaven and earth, she has no idea what to do.

Teresa uses metaphors of water and light. "It is like rain falling from the heavens into a river or a spring. There is nothing but water belonging to the river from which it fell from heaven. It is impossible to divide or separate the water belonging to the river. In my room there were two large windows trough which the light streamed in. It all becomes one." (Ibid., p. 244)

Nothing is impossible for one who loves. Teresa assumes that God works through us human instruments. She accepts imagination as a human capacity used by God. God is beyond human control. Faith is certain. The seventh mansion is the calm before the storm. Teresa bears witness to the possibility of enduring passionate love. She had her first mystical experience when she was forty years old. She had served as a nun for twenty years. Before her death, she reported, "The imaginary visions have ceased, but I always have an intellectual vision of the three persons of God. (Ibid., p. 252)

The joy through mourning rises from coming closer to the beloved and frustration from being distant. Human lovers are highly motivated to act in ways that promote closeness. "This joy is the consequence of the relentless emotional imperialism of love. The world becomes a pale shadow. Love reigns in sovereignty." (Ibid, p. 257)

Joy bombs explode. Marriage has the potential to be the epitome of communion. Marital love peaks in human communion. Woman and man were created together. When God made this climatic move, God created both in a single breath. Both were created in the image of God. Read Genesis 1:27.

We are in God's image despite our human bodies, not as bodies. Adam was an individual person in his own right. She was in her own right in communion with him. Humans need to be individuals in their own right. A single person is the image of God.

Everything right and good in creation will not be destroyed but enhanced in the kingdom of God.

Women will be women in heaven. One cannot help wondering what kind of dull creature a heavenly sexless female would be. Joy will explode. It will be more exciting than it ever was on earth. I can enjoy talking with a woman in my local grocery store or my bank without reference to her sex. I commune with her functionally, not personally. The instant I have a personal relationship with a woman, I relate to her as a male to a female person. In the example of a bank clerk, it does not involve her femaleness at all.

"The joy of the Lord" enhances courage for diving fully into life. Our imperfect love is a form of the love of God which is perfect. Sustaining imperfect love is a miracle. Love by itself is not enough.

Only with commitment will humans stay together and try again. Only with commitment will imperfect love be sufficient. Only with commitment will we bless one other with full humanness. Only with commitment will we risk deep soul to soul communication. Only with commitment will we find the courage to dive fully into life. Only wit commitment will be brave in our dying days. Give that imperfect love. Commit to a loving relationship. Work at love. Embrace the mysterious love of God that is beyond our human understanding.

Human love needs commitment. It is the glue of oneness. Receive the blessing of committed love. Keep the words to the hymn, "Everything Possible," exploding in your heart. "The only measure of your words and your deeds, will be the love you leave behind when you are done."

Eternal joy is connected to the fact we will die. Joy happens between us. The experience of joy reveals our capacity for joy. Joy is possible in the midst of difficulty. Delight is a common word.

Delight can mean "of light" or "without life. Daily delights surprise me. Sweet little interactions don't have to happen.

Joy is necessary for human well-being. Few of those who read my books, hear me teach and preach about joy. Joy cannot be ignored. We can't understand spirituality and human connections without it. We cannot understand others unless we understand joy. Joy points beyond itself to something mysteriously deeper. By communicating about joy, our souls are opened.

Joy is the fabric of spiritual reality. Maybe traditional religious people stay silent because joy transcends how we perceive life. Joy is increasingly absent in contemporary culture.

Joy is relatively independent of happiness. We must be clear of what joy is. There has never been an easy definition of joy. Some definitions of joy are vague. Joy is a response to a good object. Parishioners and students and married adults want to see the connection of joy to the whole of life now and in our future.

A model of joy may include a singular event with hints of much larger purposes. I believe joy is a durable condition. Joy matters.

Joy ignites the desire to understand why joy is so special in the plan of God. Ultimately, joy must be experienced.

Spend time out in nature. We have a park and a hiking trail in Elmwood. Look at your life. Work to put yourself in the path of joy. Our earthly journey is only the beginning. Our story is far from over. There are more chapters to include s we thrive to finish well. We continue to play a part. The work of God is not done yet.

And neither is our work. There is so much living to be done. There is more joy ahead than anyone could ever imagine. We are messengers, ministers of joy to this world. We can expect more joys. We have been given resurrection lives. We are here to live out God's story of redemption. We will join in God's wildly extravagant love in the world. Humans are tempted to write their own endings for the incomplete stories. We can't stand the loose endings.

Resurrection is about the mysterious ending to Jesus' story. Resurrection means turning back to God. Resurrection makes things right. The story does not end with the empty tomb. This is the beginning part. Resurrection is not the conclusion of the saga. Christ and we have been bruised and blooded by the darkness of earthly existence.

Jesus became frustrated with his disciples. They just didn't get it. Feel his anguish as he cries out, "Do you have eyes but fail to see? Do you have ears but fail to hear? His disciples failed to understand again and again.

I re-read at least two of my journals each year. I also enjoy seeing the years of photos that show the events of my life and ministry. I am reminded of forgotten bits of my life story. Light appears in the dark that helps me see the big picture of what I am writing about in the moment.

Bursts of joy surround me as I inject God's truth that I am a unique expression of divine joy. My exuberance bursts forth as spontaneous gratitude for my life. At other times, I share and express joy quietly. I discover a place to be alone. I reflect upon the gentle sense of well-being. With grace, I move through life with greater harmony. The spirit of joy stirs deep within me. In joy I can't help myself from extending my own joy by talking, writing, and touching others.

It would be tremendous insight if you could find ways to trigger joy. In my years of research, I have gathered thousands of suggestions. My writing is a trigger for my joy. The first thing I have been doing each morning is to write for you and for God.

A hug for my wife Laurel brings delight. I usually close my eyes when I hug her. Our hugs are not just ordinary. Ours are spontaneous, tight squeezing and full of the realization that we have each other.

My recipe for joy is to express kindness into my day. I wake up in the morning grateful that I have another day. I incorporate a random act of kindness into the time. I the evening, I express appreciation for the day.

I focus on the coming shimmering garden of delight as I am restored to God's grace and glory. Joy is the heart of our desires. As we repent, we shout for joy. Earthly joy is bound by the constraint of time. Those who find strength in eternal joy find no lasting enjoyment in worldly enjoyments because in joy we touch, feel, see, and taste are temporal. God gave every created human an appetite for joy. God in love and joy has provided satisfaction for our appetites. Read Psalm 16:11.

Being in a healthy spiritual state, we can rejoice in God. The joys of time cannot satisfy an undying truth. We are not left to search for joy. Joy is brought to our doors by the love of God. We are not left to wander among unsatisfying things. We are glad for God making us t be immortal spirits. Joy springs from God. The attributes of God become well-springs of joy to the committed believer, the thoughtful person. Jesus taught us that the attributes of God can be ours. , loving me with an unconditional, everlasting life. God is eternal. Our tears overflow with joy. God fills our souls with the deep, mysterious, unutterable bliss. One word out of heaven excelled all words. These excelling words are, "God my Father." Admiring the character and works, we know God is in me. God has grasped us with the hand of powerful love.

Joy is found in the believer who lives near to God. He is close to God with a deep realization of reconciliation to God. For the infinite to love an indignant creature, a shadow that declines. For God to have mercy on me is a marvel. God really loves me. God's love is matchless.

God stands while others fall. God sings as others weep. God grants us inward joy which comes from real strength. That strength bears fruit. Preaching is sowing. Prayer is watering. Praise is the harvest. We are like the bird that quivers in song. We are like a flower which pours forth its perfume because it does nothing else. We remember our sins and corruption. We mourn it. We share the world's troubles, and we lament with God. Joy is the perfect work of Christ. Joy leads to family happiness. For the Christian family joy is not confined to only one or two family members. Do what leads to love in your marriage and family. Learn as much about God as we can. Couples need a half-hour of prayer. Prayer is an intimate sharing between friends.

I own scores of notebooks for journaling, keeping notes on my continuing education courses, and where my journey takes me. I love the sight and smell of a brand-new notebook. When I wrote about walking in the garden with God, I was reminding of the joys of flowers and plants. I smile in a little joy.

Watching the squirrels in my own backyard and in the park outside my office window triggers. I wonder where they go. The dance and run around trees with each other. They are risky and daring. Some die under the wheels of passing cars and trucks. Storing nuts in their cheeks, they give me giggles of delight.

Decluttering our house sparks joy in me. To see my office cleared of waste and swiped out of dirt is a fun view. Laurel and I appreciate our home as a sanctuary.

Taking a walk jogs me of the beauty of our neighborhood and nature. I enjoy touching the bark on trees, watching frogs jump off logs in a pond. I disconnect my thoughts.

Helping somebody solve a problem blesses me more than it blesses those I want to help. I love to give guidance that triggers joy.

There are at least a million little ways that trigger joy. What a burst to life that is!

Joy and love and not just slushy words. Joy is not a passive feeling. Triggering joy is my vocation. I have been given a call to play a part in God's story. Joy is mine when a person says following a sermon or a new book, "Something you said about the joy of your salvation has burst out joy in me. I believe in Jesus. My whole life has been transformed."

I stroll through Elmwood Park's nature trail. I open my collections of quotes. I thumb back through my journals. I list the stories I want to tell. I pray about how my writing can encourage somebody. When I follow a well-reasoned outline and the topics for each chapter, I sometimes miss the point. As an INFJ personality type, I must do my writing in solitude. With the calming quiet, I touch the things that are lodged deep inside me.

Another INFJ, Vincent van Gogh, said, "In spite of everything I shall rise again: I will take my pencil, which I have forsaken in my times of great discouragement, and I will go on with my drawing."

If an artist dwells on what publishers, editors, and book buyers will judge what you have written, somebody asks you to preach or to talk about some situation they need you to help with. The normal urge to get up and go is a temptation to leave to do what is begging your attention and time.

Now I want to share the most important thoughts about separation from God in any soul. People take little account of the life of the soul. The illusions of temptation capture our attention. Some devote more and more energy to the things of this world. As couples carefully provide for family, honor their vows, and serve neighbors, we compromise with the allure of sin. Encounters and actions that previous generations considered sin and weakness are now pursued. Greed is an accepted part of our work or business. We cheat. We lie. We lust. We gossip. We trash reputations. Marriage and family are disposable. Marriage and home were the center of our commitment. Today many show less regard for the dignity of human life. Lack of respect for the sabbath is commonplace. Each sinful choice does incredible injury to the soul. That is what is limiting the possibility for the joys of salvation.

God does not want any of us to suffer eternal damnation. Rejecting God's grace is to condemn ourselves for eternity and deprive us from the vision of God. Rejection of God becomes irrevocable after we die. Read Matthew 7:13-14. We choose hell wit the decisions we make in life. God is love. God never overrides human freedom or forcibly dispels our free will. We must seek refuge in Christ.

The merits of Christ are the only, all-sufficient means for salvation. Christ Jesus has made atonement and satisfaction for all sin. Jesus calls us to share the Kingdom of heaven. For us human beings, heaven is a place fille wit the fullness of communion wit God in eternal life. We will see God face to face and live with our God forever. The perfect union with our creator satisfies our deepest longing.

The vision and love of God will bring infinite joy to the justified. We will encounter the reality of the glorified Blessed Trinity. It is the ultimate end and fulfillment of the deepest human longings. The redeemed from all times and places unite in union with Christ in the communion of the saints. We cannot see God unless through divine grace and the light of glory unites us and gives the capacity to receive.

Joy is the crown of a life well-lived. All the powers of every universe will bow to Christ, the saved will be irradiated by the light of Christ. Read Isaiah 25:6-8. The joy of our salvation is not the negation of space or time. Freedom will operate. There will be an unimaginable superabundance of the spaces and times with the fullness of joy with God.

When Mississippi State won the 2021 national title in the College World Series in Omaha, I was intrigued by their discipline. One player had a length of strong rubber bands with one end connected to an iron post and the other connected to his wrist. He swung his arms and hands slowly. He visualized swinging through the strike zone. This Bulldog player was not holding a bat. Mississippi State had the power to hit home runs. Most of time they prepared for hitting the ball. Small ball coaches call it. Another player is hitting baseballs off a tee. Fifty swings. The soft toss was done by a coach sitting down with a bucket of balls. Slowly each ball was tossed into the strike zone. The player hit each ball like a kid hits the ball in tee ball leagues. By the time the team played in the massive baseball stadium to hit three or four times with four dozen swings, State diamond players had practiced their swing more than five hundred times.

Good writers write something every day. One secret to Mississippi's wins in the World Series, and winning the two out of three games final over Vanderbilt, the defending champion, was that they worked on their craft every day.

When Vanderbilt made their last out in the ninth inning, joy exploded.

More than 25,000 fans from Starkville, Mississippi traveled to Omaha to cheer Mississippi State as they won their first national college championship in any sport.

The explosion of joy brought tears to the entire crowd. Tears of disappointment flowed from the Vanderbilt fans. Tears of upmost delight for Mississippi's miracle lasted for days.

AFTERWORD

With superb storytelling and precise thought, James McReynolds writes a beautiful portrait of the marital relationship. This is not just another book seeking to dismantle the facets of marriage and how couples can discover joy. Dr. McReynolds has given my wife and I a vision of what marriage can be.

The reader faces the dilemma of how brief life is and suggestions for our loss of a spouse or close family member. He proves to be a gifted guide as he walks his readers through philosophical depths and theological mountains. He offers numerous fresh insights and helpful reflections.

Purpose, meaning, and goals are rewards enough. James' book is one of the few books I will re-read. Countless couples and single adults will be enabled to navigate the painful and joyful waters of life. He takes the fear out of death, for it is a gateway to eternal life. He faithfully writes of our ultimate destiny, giving hope to those who mourn.

In this inspiring book, he gives us an eternal embrace of God for God's children. This volume will open minds and souls to the gift of God, eternal life, and love for Jesus the Christ.

James has achieved something extraordinary. I couldn't put his book down. This work is on a profound subject. He writes with rich clarity, faith, hope, and joy with a warm personal witness from himself, and his wife Laurel. They are pleasingly vulnerable as he describes a marriage that many couples can never achieve. He invites us to travel on a uniquely personal and brilliantly crafted journey with a faithful committed couple who have created a life full of daring acts of intimacy, endless searching for fun and oneness.

I am grateful and my spouse and I have conquered tradition and inhibition. This book has allowed us to become aware of Christ's presence in our lives. Our tears have been converted into laughter. Through this book, we have touched joy while surrounded by Christ and transformed by healing love.

-- Kenneth Johansson, M.D.
Dallas, Texas

BIBLIOGRAPHY

Achtemeier, Elizabeth. *The Committed Marriage*. Philadelphia: Westminster Press, 1976.

Allbritton, Cliff. *How to Get Married and Stay That Way*. Nashville: Broadman Press, 1982.

Alther, Lisa. *Original Sins*. New York: Knopf, 1981.

Augsburger, David. *Caring Enough to Confront*. Glendale, California: Regal Books, 1989.

Backus, William and Chapian, Marie. *Telling Yourself the Truth*. Minneapolis: Bethany House Publishers, 1980.

Bakke, Dennis. *Joy at Work: A Revolutionary Approach to Fun on the Job*. Seattle: PVG Publishers, 2008.

Barback, Lonnie and Geisinger, David. *Going the Distance*. New York: Doubleday, 1991.

Barr, Browne. *Never Too Late to Be Loved: How One Couple Under Stress Discovered Intimacy and Joy*. Shippensburg, Pennsylvania: Ragged Edge Press, 1998.

Belliveau, Fred. *Understanding Sexual Inadequacy*. New York: Bantom Books, 1988.

Biddle, Perry H. *The Goodness of Marriage*. Nashville: The Upper Room, 1989.

Birren, James E. and Deutchman, Donna. *Guiding Autobiography Groups for Older Adults:
Exploring the Fabric of Life*. Baltimore: Johns Hopkins University Press, 1995.

Blanchard, Kenneth and Johnson, Spencer. *The One Minute Manager*. New York: Berkley Publishers, 1983.

Blanchard, Kenneth and Peale, Norman Vincent. *The Power of Ethical Management*. New York: William Morrow and Company, 1988.

Blumstein, Philip, and Schwartz, Pepper. *American Couples*. New York: Morrow Press, 1983.

Bonhoeffer, Dietrich. *Letters and Papers from Prison.* Translation of 90 volumes. Minneapolis: Fortress Press, 1994.

Bovet, Theodor. *A Handbook to Marriage.* Garden City: Dolphin Books, 1970.

Brooks, David. *The Second Mountain: Quest for a Moral Life.* New York: Random House, 2019.

Brooks, David and Volf, Miroslav, "A Life Worth Living," webinar at Yale University Divinity School, July 28, 2021.

Bugen, Larry A. *Love and Renewal: A Couple's Guide to Commitment.* Oakland: New Harbinger Publications, 1998.

Burgess, E.W. *The Romantic Impulse and Family Disorganization.* New York: Survey Press, 1954.

Butterfield, Oliver M. *Sexual Harmony in Marriage.* Buchanan, New York: Emerson Books, 1981.

Comfort, Alex. *The Joy of Sex.* New York: Crown Books, 1972.

Crane, Christopher A. and Hamel, Michael. *Effective Influence: Impacting Your Workplace for Christ.* Colorado Springs: NavPress, 1999.

Douty, Linda. *How Can I Let Go If I Don't Know If I Am Hanging On?* Harrisburg, Pennsylvania: Morehouse Press, 2005.

Fincham, F.D., Beach, S.R., Lambert, Nathan, and Braithwaite. "Spiritual Behaviors and Relationship Satisfaction: A Critical Analysis of the Role of Prayer," *Journal of Clinical and Social Psychology,* 27, 362-388, 2008.

Fromm, Erich. *To Have or to Be.* New York: Bantam Books, 1976.

Gallagher, S. K. *Evangelical Identity and Gendered Family Life.* Piscataway, New Jersey: Rutgers University Press, 2003.

Gordon, Sol. *Why Love Is Not Enough.* Boston: Bob Adams, Inc., 1988.

Grauman, Brigid. "Healthy, Healthy, and Odd: Nonconformists Live Longer," *The Wall Street Journal,* November 2, 1995.

Guinness, Oz. *The Call: Finding Purpose and Fulfilling the Central Purpose of Your Life*. Nashville: World Publishing Company, 1998.

Hailes, John. "Sexuality and Aging," *Social Biology Research Center Bulletin*, volume 4, number 3, Melbourne, Australia, 1980.

Howell, John C. *Equality and Submission in Marriage*. Nashville: Broadman Press, 1979.

Julian of Norwich. *Revelations of Divine Love*. Trans. Elizabeth Spearing. New York: Penguin, 1998.

Kaplan, H.S. *Disorders of Sexual Desire*. New York: Simon & Schuster, 1996.

Killinger, John. *The Zacchaeus Solution: How Christians Can Reverse the World's Economic Downturn*. Cleveland, Tennessee: Parson's Porch Books, 2010.

Kingma, Daphne Rose. *True Love: How to Make Your Relationship Sweeter, Deeper, and More Passionate*. Berkley, California: Conari Press, 1996.

Kipling, Rudyard. *Classic Poems*. New York: Random House, 2006.

Kitzinger, Sheila. *Woman's Experience of Sex*. New York: G.P. Putnam's Sons, Inc., 1983.

Komarovsky, Mirra. *Blue Collar Marriages*. New York: Vintage Press, 1967.

Lee, John A. *The Colors of Love*. New York: Bantam, 1977.

Lidell, Lucinda. *The Sensual Body*. New York: Simon and Schuster, 1983

Mace, David R. *Close Companions*. New York: Continuum, 1985.

McGinnis, Alan Loy. *The Romance Factor*. New York: Harper and Row, 1982.

McReynolds, James. *Joy Comes in the Mourning: Love Is Forever*. Cleveland, Tennessee: Parson's Porch Books, 2020.

McReynolds, James. *The Spirituality of Joy: The Least Discussed Human Emotion*. Cleveland, Tennessee: Parson's Porch Books, 2011.

McReynolds, James. *Joy in All Seasons: Walking Each Other Home to God.* Cleveland, Tennessee: Parson's Porch Books, 2021.

Miller, Calvin. *The Empowered Leader: Ten Keys to Servant Leadership.* Nashville: Broadman and Holman Publishers, 1995.

Moore, Thomas. *Soul Mates.* New York: Harper/Collins, 1994.

Murray, Wendy, "The Radical Vision of Saint Clare's Radical Spiritual Vision," *The Christian Century,* Vol. 138 (July 28, 2021) pp. 22-25.

Neddleman, Jacob. *Money and the Meaning of Life.* New York: Doubleday, 1993.

Knight, George W. *The New Testament Teaching of the Role Relationship of Men and Women.* Grand Rapids: Baker Book House, 1977.

Nouwen, Henri, "All Is Grace," *Weavings: A Journal of the Christian Spiritual Life,* 7, number 6 (November 1992) pp. 39-40.

Oates, Wayne. *When You Can't Find Time for Each Other.* Saint Meinrad, Indiana: Abbey Press, 1982.

Offit, Avodah. *Night Thoughts: Reflections of a Sex Therapist.* New York: Congdon and Weed.
1996.

Oliver, Mary, "The Summer Day," *New and Selected Poems.* Boston: Beacon Press, 1992.

Onedera, J.D. *The Role of Religion in Marriage and Family Counseling.* New York: Routledge Books, 2008.

Pargament, K.I. *Spiritually Integrated Psychotherapy: Understanding and Addressing the Sacred.* New York: Guilford Press, 2007.

Phillips, Michael. *The Seven Laws of Money.* New York: Random House, 1974.

Pincus, Lily. *Death and the Family.* New York: Random House, 1978.

Pines, Ayala. *Keeping the Spark Alive.* New York: Saint Martin's Press, 1988.

Porter, Sylvia. *Sylvia Porter's New Money Book for Married People*. New York: Doubleday, 1989.

Powell, John. *The Secret of Staying in Love*. Allen, Texas: Argus Communications, 1979.

Reid, Clyde. *Celebrate the Temporary*. New York: Harper and Row, 1972.

Reuben, David. *Everything You Always Wanted to Know About Sex but Were Afraid to Ask*. New York: Bantam, 1973.

Richmond, Gary. *An Ounce of Prevention: Safeguarding Your Marriage*. 13 video sessions. Leader's Guide. Fullerton, California: First Evangelical Free Church, 2003.

Romney, Ronna and Harrison, Beppie. *Giving Time a Chance*. New York: M. Evans and Company, 1987.

Rubin, Zack. "Measurement of Romantic Love," *Journal of Personality and Social Psychology*, 15, pp. 343-355, 1979.

Saussy, Carroll. *The Art of Growing Old: A Guide to Faithful Aging*. Minneapolis: Augsburg Fortress Publishing, 1998.

Satir, Virginia. *Peoplemaking*. Palo Alto, California: Science and Behavior Books, Inc., 1972.

Saward, John. *Sweet and Blessed Country: The Christian Hope for Heaven*. Oxford, England: Oxford University Press, 2008.

Scitovsky, T. J. *Human Desire and Economic Satisfaction: Essays on the Frontiers of Economics*. New York: New York University Press, pp. 183-203, 1988.

Seymour, Robert E. *Aging without Apology: Living the Senior Years with Integrity and Faith*. Valley Forge, Pennsylvania: Judson Press, 1996.

Shinabarger, Jeffrey. *Yes or No: How Your Everyday Decisions Will Forever Shape Your Life*. Colorado Springs: David C. Cook, 2014.

Smedes, Lewis. *Sex for Christians*. Grand Rapids, Michigan: William W. Eerdmans Publishing Company, 1994.

Snyder, Gary. *The Practice of the Wild.* San Francisco: North Point Press, 1990.

Sternburg, Robert and Barnes, Michael, editors, *The Psychology of Love.* New Haven and London: Yale University Press, 1988.

Stevens, Velma. *After Weeping a Song.* Nashville: Broadman Press, 1980.

Stockton, Shreve. *Meditations with Cows: What I've Learned from Daisy.* New York. Teacher Perigee, imprint of Random House, 2021.

Sullender, R. Scott. *Losses in Later Life: A New Way of Walking with God.* New York: Paulist Press, 1999.

Taylor, Barbara Brown. *Leaving Church: A Memoir of Faith.* New York: Harper/Collins, 2006.

Teresa of Avila. *The Collected Works of Saint Teresa of Avila.* Trans. Kieran Kavanaugh and Otilio Rodriguez. Washington, D.C.: ICS Publications, 1978.

Teresa of Avila. *Story of a Soul: The Autobiography of Saint Teresa of Lisieux.* Trans. John Clarke. Washington, D.C.: ICS Publications, 1979.

Teresa of Avila. *Saint Teresa: Her Last Conversations.* Trans. John Clarke. Washington, D.C.: ICS Publications, 1980.

Tournier, Paul. *To Understand Each Other.* Richmond, Virginia: John Knox Press, 1967.

Van Cappellen, Peter. "Rethinking Self-Transcendent Positive Emotions and Religion: Insights from Psychological and Biblical Research, "*Psychology of Religion and Spirituality,* 9(3), pp. 254-264.

Viscott, David. *How to Live* with *Another Person.* New York: Pocket Books Publishing, 1976.

Waggener, Richard. *Marriage Enrichment.* Nashville: Baptist Marriage Enrichment System, 1981.

Watkins, P.C. and Emmons, R.A. "Joy Is a Distinct Positive Emotion: An Assessment of Joy and Its Relationship to Gratitude and Well-Being," *The Journal of Positive Psychology, 13(5), pp. 522-539.*

Webb, Lance. *Making Love Grow*. Nashville: Upper Room, 1984.

Weeks, David and James, Jamie. *Eccentrics: A Study of Sanity and Strangeness*. New York: Villard Books, 1995.

Wright, Norman. *Seasons of Marriage*. Ventura, California: Regal Books, 1982.

Zuckerman, Mike. *Sensation Seeking: Beyond the Optimal Level of Arousal*. Hillsdale, New Jersey: Erlbaum Printers, 1996.

NOTES ABOUT THE AUTHOR

James McReynolds and his wife Laurel have been married for 35 years. Four children and six grandchildren are in the family. They now have four great grandchildren. They have conducted Family Life Conferences in churches, and the National Family Life "Weekends to Remember," sponsored by Campus Crusade for Christ. Together they have shared family therapy, coaching, and counseling with families.

Dr. McReynolds is an associate member of the American Association of Marriage and Family Therapists. He is a charter member of the American Association of Christian Counselors. He wrote numerous articles for *The Christian Single*, a magazine published by the Sunday School Board of the Southern Baptist Convention in Nashville. He has used his counseling gifts as a licensed mental health practitioner in Tennessee and Nebraska. He earned the doctor of psychology degree at Oxford University. He has five doctorates and nine degrees.

He earned his D.Div. at Vanderbilt University Divinity School, M.R.Ed. from Midwestern Baptist Theological Seminary in Kansas City. Dr. McReynolds earned a B. Jour at the University of Missouri-Columbia. His B.A. was from Carson-Newman University in Tennessee. He served as a graduate assistant in psychology of religion at Baylor University in Texas.

Laurel McReynolds earned her B.S. and. R.N. at Nebraska Wesleyan University in Lincoln and Clarkson School of Nursing in Omaha. She did graduate studies in family counseling at the University of Nebraska-Lincoln. She finished Rouxbe Online Culinary. She enjoys cooking schools in Savannah, Georgia; Lincoln and Omaha, and a cooking school with Faye Hess at the Chateau des Sablons in France. She has travel throughout Europe enjoying the tours with the Joy of Music organist Diane Bish.

She is music director for Saint Paul United Methodist Church, Elmwood and Ebenezer United Methodist Church in Murdock. Laurel has enjoyed playing the piano and organ, the harp, handbells, marimba, and any tool for providing her gift of music. Her choir has held Joy of Music concerts for church choirs in Cass County, Nebraska for many years.

Laurel was selected as Miss Murdock and Miss Cass County. She enjoys reading, movies, music concerts, and selected television.

James and Laurel are active in retirement. They live in a custom-designed new home in Elmwood, Nebraska. Both love the feeling of coming home. Traveling from their comfortable home, they have shared joy throughout the world. His ministry and writing have been a balancing blend of scholarship and emotional intensity. They also feel at home with themselves.

They enjoy who they are and where they are and what they are doing. Their spiritual oneness reminds them that they are pilgrims who will one day live in the eternal city with God.

In a time when traditional publishing is in transition and turmoil, he is passionate, along with his publisher, in helping others share their stories. God has given Jim a gift for writing. Writing has become his mission in life.

What many people call impossible, James labels it a challenge. Opportunities that others walk away from, he runs towards. The freeing message from his books is that no matter the circumstances, you can experience joy.

James brings fresh air for those who may have given up on their marriage and the church. His wisdom is the result of decades of vulnerable ministry in local congregations and in churches throughout the world.

www.ingramcontent.com/pod-product-compliance
Lightning Source LLC
Chambersburg PA
CBHW071451070526
44578CB00001B/311